Family Business
Governance

Family Business Governance

Increasing Business Effectiveness and Professionalism

Keanon J. Alderson, MBA, PhD

BEP BUSINESS EXPERT PRESS

Family Business Governance: Increasing Business Effectiveness and Professionalism
Copyright © Business Expert Press, LLC, 2019.

First published in 2019 by
Business Expert Press, LLC
222 East 46th Street, New York, NY 10017
www.businessexpertpress.com

ISBN-13: 978-1-94999-130-7 (paperback)
ISBN-13: 978-1-94999-131-4 (e-book)

Business Expert Press Entrepreneurship and Small Business Management Collection

Collection ISSN: 1946-5653 (print)
Collection ISSN: 1946-5661 (electronic)

Cover and interior design by S4Carlisle Publishing Services Private Ltd., Chennai, India

First edition: 2019

10 9 8 7 6 5 4 3 2 1

Printed in the United States of America.

Dedication

To my family,
Sandy, Sean, Courtney, Cassandra, Dana, Jeren, Aurelia,
and the grandchildren not here yet.

Abstract

Family business is the most prevalent form of business organization in the world. Much of the existing literature on family and corporate governance focuses on the larger and often publicly owned corporations instead of the unique and special issues of the much more prevalent privately held (usually smaller) family businesses. This book presents research-based information to provide the reader a deeper understanding of the complex nature of family-owned businesses, their problems and challenges, and the unique governance structures and mechanisms that have been developed to properly guide a family business to greater effectiveness. For the family, such structures include having family meetings, a family council, and a family constitution. For the business, the board of directors provides experienced and knowledgeable advice and recommendations, as well as oversight and monitoring activities. For the owners, a shareholder's council and an annual shareholder meeting allow increased communication and voting on decisions. These family governance mechanisms have been shown to increase communication, reduce conflict, and improve decision making and professionalism. Each governance tool will be explored in depth. The audience for this book is family business owners, consultants, practitioners, and family business scholars. Cases provide readers an opportunity to apply their learning to real business problems.

Keywords

family firm governance; family business; family-owned enterprise; family business governance; firm performance; board of directors; governance; family council; family constitution; management; transparency; professionalism; corporate social responsibility

Contents

Preface

I became interested in the subject of family business after working as a partner in my family's business when I was younger. I worked with my parents and brother for 17 years.

We did not have a successful succession of leadership to the second generation. Instead, we received a buyout offer, sold the business, and went our separate ways. More recently, I have employed my children in my own family business along with my wife. I studied family business decision making during my doctoral work and wrote my dissertation on the subject.

I still miss our family business. When in agreement, we could make lightning fast decisions and be implementing them within minutes. This enabled us to compete very successfully with several very large corporations in our industry. However, I wish we had been familiar with the principles of family and business governance. We could have benefitted from a family council. Family members could have had an outlet to air their views and participate in decision making. A board of advisors would have provided us with recommendations based on knowledge and experience.

Keanon Alderson
March 14, 2019

Acknowledgments

This book is a continuation of my first book *Understanding the Family Business: The differences between family and non-family businesses (2018)*. In teaching my family business classes as well as performing research and consulting with family firms, it seems most of the family-owned firms could benefit by having an increased emphasis on governance. Many of the problems could have been prevented and/or managed by better governance procedures. This book explains in detail how to use governance tools as well as why and when. For example, the age-old problem of succession can be discussed sooner by having a family council and by the creation of a family constitution. Proper governance can help professionalize the family-owned firm.

I wish to thank California Baptist University for granting me a sabbatical to have the time to perform the research and write the draft of this book. I thank my students for their encouragement and tough questions.

I also want to thank my acquisitions editor at Business Expert Press Rob Zwettler for encouraging the publication of this book. Thanks to Charlene Kronstedt and Sheri Dean at BEP for answering all my questions. Thanks go out to the Entrepreneurship and Small Business collection guest editor Scott Shane. I would also like to thank Rene Caroline and her team for excellent copyediting and book production.

Prologue

What Is Governance?

There are various definitions of corporate governance. The definition depends on the particular situation of each business, suggesting firms may use different governance structures based on the size of the firm and whether the firm is publicly or privately held (Huse and Landström 2002).

Corporate governance involves a set of relationships between a company's management, its board, its shareholders, and other stakeholders. Corporate governance also provides the structure through which the objectives of the company are set, and the means of attaining those objectives and monitoring performance are determined. Good corporate governance should provide proper incentives for the board and management to pursue objectives that are in the interests of the company and its shareholders and should facilitate effective monitoring (OCED 2007).

Sir Alan Cadbury is the most noted governance scholar. He provides a simple definition: A system by which companies are directed and controlled (Cadbury 1999). The governance of a family firm is more complex than nonfamily firms. Family as well as business relationships need to be considered (Cadbury 2000).

In summary, the governance (how a company is directed and controlled) of a family firm is more complicated than a nonfamily firm. Nonfamily firms focus mainly on corporate governance. As we will discuss further in this book, there are three areas of governance in a family firm: governance of the business (corporate), governance of the family, and ownership governance.

PART I

Overview of Family Business

CHAPTER 1

Introduction to Family Business

Before discussing family and corporate governance, the reader should have some basic background knowledge in family business, and public and private business ownership. The following section is designed as a quick primer or refresher on need-to-know information that allows readers to be knowledgeable when presented with family business terms, mechanisms, and issues that can be prevented by and/or solved with more effective governance.

Throughout the world, family business is the most prevalent form of business. It is as much as 70 percent of all firms in the United States (Astrachan and Shanker 2003) and an even higher amount in Europe. Of the many companies today, chances are they started with family support and resources such as patient financial capital or low-cost family employees. Many companies would not exist without the influence and involvement of the founders' families.

Most family firms throughout the world exist as small and medium-sized enterprises, (SMEs). Many family businesses make a conscious and deliberate decision to stay small. They purposely do this to stay in control, make decisions as they desire, avoid the numerous problems of growing larger and more complex, and still make an excellent living. Some of these companies eventually scale up to become large corporations. The founders may decide to access outside financial capital through an initial public offering (IPO) and sell shares to the public. Of the companies that make up Standard & Poor's (S&P) 500 Index, fully one-third are considered family businesses. The same is true for the Fortune 500 list of America's largest public corporations (Anderson and Reeb 2003).

Millions of small family businesses exist all over the world. These families increase their standard of living by being business owners. They feed and clothe their families, pay the rent or mortgage on their homes, and send their children to school with the resources of the family business. They employ people and add to the local economy. Some businesses have been in the family for multiple generations. They are a significant factor in every country's economy and contribute to significant employment growth.

The Answer to Increasing the Professionalism of the Family Business

A major criticism of family businesses is that many are perceived to be unprofessional. They are called small and "mom-and-pop's." Many people believe they are not managed in an effective manner. They are considered not "business like." In some cases, the criticisms are true. The answer to many of these criticisms is instituting effective governance. By establishing effective governance structures, it helps increase the professionalism of a family business. Governance is key to formalizing procedures, increasing communication, increasing transparency to all stakeholders, making logical and rational decisions without emotion, and providing tools and techniques for the proper management of a firm.

Privately Held Firms

A company that has not sold stock to outsiders larger than a select group of individuals is known as a privately held company. It is privately owned. An interested investor cannot call their stockbroker and buy stock in the firm. Because it is private, the company can make all decisions on its own without any outside input or constraints. The business does not have to comply with the same Securities and Exchange Commission (SEC) regulations as a publicly held firm would. Most family-owned businesses are privately held. They have total freedom to act in their best interest, or, as is the case with altruistic behavior, to not act in their best interest. However, it is the family's decision alone to decide how to act, what goals to pursue, and what opportunities to seize, without needing to consult any public shareholders or outside stakeholders.

An example of a privately held large family corporation is Hobby Lobby. This company is completely owned by David Green and his family. Another example is Enterprise Holdings Inc., the owner of Enterprise Rent-A-Car and 100 percent owned by the Taylor family. It is the largest private owner of automobiles in the world. A private investor is not able to buy stock in either corporation because they are privately held and not public.

Publicly Held Firms

A company that has sold stock to the public and is listed on a stock exchange is considered by the SEC to be a publicly held company. The company must have a board of directors (BOD), report their financial statements publicly, and do so in a timely manner. The company is managed by upper management: the chief executive officer (CEO), chief operating officer (COO), chief financial officer (CFO), and president of the corporation. The BOD provides oversight to management, has legal authority to act for the benefit of shareholders, and has significant legal liability if they do not do so in an ethical and responsible manner. The board has the power to hire and terminate the CEO.

The introduction of Sarbanes–Oxley (Sarbox) financial accountability requirements was a sea change in corporate governance. It tightened up requirements for publicly held companies and instituted much more transparency and reporting. Directors of the organization now have legal liability when sitting on the BOD rather than being a mere figurehead. The legislation required boards be restructured to include outsiders rather than a board full of company insiders and yes men.

Facebook, Google, and Netflix are all public companies. Examples of large publicly held *and* family-controlled firms are Ford Motor Company, still controlled by the Ford family for over a century, and Walmart, controlled by the Walton family. The general public could buy stock in these companies if they desired.

Definition of Family Business

It is unfortunate that family business researchers have been unable to arrive at an agreed-upon definition of what is and is not a family-owned business. At one time, there were 34 definitions of family business (Sharma, Chrisman, and Chua 1996), which make comparisons and generalizations between various firms difficult, if not impossible. As an example, is multibillion-dollar family-controlled Walmart similar to the family-owned lawnmower shop on the corner of Main Street? It would be difficult to compare the two. However, both are considered family businesses. So, the definition is vital to understanding family business. The following lists several family business definitions:

1. Ownership control (15 percent) or higher by two or more members of a family or a partnership of families.
2. Strategic influence by family members on the management of the firm, whether by being active in management, continuing to shape culture, serving as advisors or board members, or being active shareholders.
3. Concern for family relationships.
4. The dream (or possibility) of continuity across generations.

   (Poza and Daugherty 2014, p. 7)

In a family business, a family member is the chief executive; there are at least two generations of family control; a minimum of 5 percent of the voting stock is held by family or trust interest associated with it (Colli, Fernandez-Perez, and Rose 2003).

A family business is one in which a family has enough ownership to determine the composition of the board where the CEO and at least one other executive is a family member, and where the intent is to pass the firm on to the next generation (Miller and Le Breton-Miller 2003).

The family business is a business governed and/or managed with the intention to shape and pursue the vision of the business held by a dominant coalition controlled by members of the same family or a small number of families in a manner that is potentially sustainable across generations of the family or families (Chua, Chrisman, and Sharma 1999).

Many other definitions reduce the amount of ownership required to have control over an organization and its strategies. The three main similarities between the definitions are:

- Desire to pass on to future generations.
- Ability to exert its control over the company.
- Two or more members of a family or families involved.

These three items will allow a broad discussion of both *family-owned* businesses and *family-controlled* businesses in this book.

Family-*Owned* Businesses

If a founding family owns 100 percent of the stock in a privately held firm, they have what is considered a *family-owned business*. The family owns the company; they own all the stock; there are no outside-of-the-family shareholders. The family is free to make *all* the decisions themselves and can run the company any way they desire. There are no outsiders to tell them what to do or how to run their business. That is a key point; it is *their* business. The family has complete ownership, and thus complete control of the firm. An example of a family-owned firm would be the corner market, owned by a husband and wife and employing their children. They own 100 percent of the business.

Family-*Controlled* Businesses

If the founding family sells stock to the public and has numerous outside-the-family shareholders, it is considered a publicly owned company. The family no longer has the total freedom to run the company as they would if they owned all the stock and were privately held. The stockholders have voting rights, there needs to be transparency in communication, and all stakeholders need to be informed. The BOD has responsibility for oversight of the business to protect the shareholders and stakeholders. The board may vote against the families' wishes. The family no longer owns or runs the company outright. It is no longer completely *their* business.

However, a family, through its sheer number of shares, or with a separate class of voting shares, can effectively control a company even without full ownership. This is called *family controlled* since the family controls the firm through its ownership rights (shares of stock), through its voting rights, and often both.

Ford Motor Company is an example of a family-controlled company with a dual class or special class of shares commonly referred to as super shares or voting shares. These special "B" class shares allow voting rights of a single share to be worth many times that of common stockholder's shares. This is how the Ford family effectively controls the multibillion-dollar automotive company with only (approximately) two percent ownership of the shares yet 40 percent of the votes (Automotive News 2013). Warren Buffet–controlled Berkshire Hathaway Inc. has two classes of shares. The "A" class has 10,000 times the voting power and 1,500 times the economic interest (value) than the class "B" stock (Cunningham 2014). Buffet enjoys a larger number of votes than his ownership stake would normally consist of through his use of dual class stock. Another example of a family-controlled firm is privately held Koch Industries, where the Koch family owns 84 percent of the stock. With this outright majority of the stock, they control the firm.

When there are large individual stockholders in a firm, those stockholders wield significant power and influence. They may select and recommend members for the BOD who are "family-friendly" insiders. Through the BOD, they can influence the board (by their number of favorable directors) and management and set the strategy and direction of the firm. In the case of the Koch family, only 16 percent of a dissenting view could ever oppose their wishes, which would be quickly outvoted.

The Walton family owns 41 percent of the stock of publicly held Walmart. If the family votes as a group, their 41 percent stake is larger than any other major shareholder. Because the firm is publicly owned, there are numerous individual stockholders. It would be nearly impossible to get the hundreds of thousands of individual Walmart stockholders to come together and agree on a proposal the family does not support and to outvote the family.

The Quandt family owns 41 percent of the shares outstanding of BMW. It is a public company, but the family has enough shares and thus enough votes to effectively control the company. Lastly, Cargill is a huge multibillion-dollar global company that is privately held by the Cargill and MacMillan families, who collectively control 85 percent of the firm's shares. It is important to understand the difference between a family-owned business and a family-controlled business. The governance mechanisms are often different for each.

How Family Businesses Are Different Than Nonfamily Businesses

As every family business owner knows, when they turn on the financial news they rarely, if ever, hear anything relevant concerning a company of their type of ownership. They usually hear about large publicly owned businesses. Their company is not like General Motors, or Netflix, or Apple. Their company has both unique opportunities as a family-owned business, and different and hard to manage challenges (Gersick, Davis, Hampton, and Landsberg 1997). When a family business is functioning well, there is good communication among family members, a high amount of trust, and quick decision making, which can be a tremendous competitive advantage over its competitors. Speed is a tremendous competitive advantage that well-functioning family firms possess. They can enter new markets quickly and can tie up supplier relationships with contracts and effectively bar their competitors from copying their strategy. "Quick decision making is critical in business and tight-knit families in business move fast" (Poza and Daugherty 2014, p. 16).

When a family business is not functioning well, it is most likely caused by lack of communication. This is commonly associated with interpersonal and dysfunctional conflict which is very disruptive and can lead to ineffective decision making. Consider a company that has problems and is slow in making decisions. It is easy to see how the company could face difficulty with strategically planning for the future. Having slow responses to changes or competitive threats to their business places the company at a competitive disadvantage that could seriously impact the company's ability to compete and win in the marketplace. This type of dysfunctional family business would most likely be reacting to situations instead of being proactive and making their competitors react to *their* moves in the marketplace. That is not a recipe for domination in the marketplace. It can be a symptom of poor governance.

When naysayers declare there is no difference between a family firm and a nonfamily firm, they do not have a complete understanding of family business. They are not aware of the unique problems and opportunities faced by families in business together. In addition, as opposed to nonfamily-owned businesses, there are governance tools and mechanisms that do not exist at nonfamily firms. To effectively thrive in the marketplace, a family-owned business needs to institute good governance practices. This is the solution to critics of so-called "unprofessional" family business.

Because of the addition of the family unit within a business, which is by far the biggest difference between family firms and nonfamily firms, there are numerous differences that nonfamily firms do not have to face. When we see a multigenerational firm that has succeeded for decades or multiple generations, it is deserving of respect. We must ask ourselves: How did they overcome all their unique challenges? How did they persevere and succeed? What can we learn from them?

An excellent example of family perseverance in the face of numerous adversities and challenges is the Italian-based Beretta Firearms Company. They are in their 15th generation of family ownership, with the 16th being groomed presently (Martin 2014). They are the oldest manufacturing company in the world. They have been taken over by the Pope, Mussolini, and then Hitler. They went through two world wars. They have never been more successful, and now have a Beretta merchandise division and sell some of the finest firearms in the world. Some are considered works of art and retail for over a hundred thousand dollars. What have they done as a family to manage through all that adversity and still be family owned?

A contrasting example is the story of the Dassler brothers and Adidas and Puma. The two brothers took over their father's shoe company. They popularized what are now known as athletic shoes. The brothers and their wives had significant interpersonal conflict that devolved into serious dysfunction. One brother broke away from the family business and started a competing athletic shoe company. The two companies were based in the same city on opposite sides. There were local bars that were restricted to Adidas workers and supporters only, and others for Puma allies.

The brothers were not on speaking terms for several decades (Smit 2008; Gordon and Nicholson 2008).

Suppose the CEO of General Motors was sued for divorce. Would the entire company be put into turmoil? Would it threaten the company's existence as a going concern? Certainly not! Now visualize the husband and wife founders of a family business getting a divorce. Their children all work at the firm. Sides would be taken, blame issued, conflict would break out, decisions would go unmade, and the disruption would be constant. This example is just one situation that makes family-owned businesses different than nonfamily businesses.

Founder Centrality

A common issue among future generations in a business is the continuing influence of the founder that rises above the entire organization, a phenomenon referred to as "founder centrality" (Crittenden, Athanassiou, and Kelly 2000, p. 27) or "generational shadow" (Davis and Harveston 1999, p. 311). Such influence can have both positive and negative factors associated with it. It helps future generations, in that they tend to follow the original mission or vision of the organization as set by the founder, including caring for long-term employees, the community, and their customers. The influence becomes negative if the successive generations are not allowed to make their own decisions or are second-guessed by a meddling founder who has not fully retired. This negative influence has been a major reason for future generational members to exit the family firm. The family council may be a way to allow the next generation of leadership to emerge from under the negative shadow of the founder.

A positive aspect of founder centrality is the superior performance seen by some founder-led organizations. This describes firms where the founder is seen to be central to the organization, such as Mark Zuckerberg at Facebook, Jeff Bezos at Amazon, Michael Dell at Dell Computers, or Elon Musk at Space X and Tesla. It is difficult to imagine these companies without their founders. The founder is *central* to the organization. In family firms, it is a necessity to consider the central influence of a family business founder on the top management team (TMT) and on the firm's strategic values, goals, and behavior (Crittenden, Athanassiou, and Kelly 2000).

Family First or Business First?

Family businesses can also be divided into two main types based on their goals. What is the purpose of the company? Is it to provide for the family? Is it to employ family members, even those who may not be very productive? This type of company is described as being *family first* (Poza and Daugherty 2014). The family comes first, before the business. In this type of business, family members benefit. They may have higher than market rate salaries and may personally benefit from cars and travel on the company. Family members often see the company as a bank and receive low interest loans when needed.

The opposing view is a *business first* business. In this type of business, the family realizes the business is number one. The business exists to benefit the family, but the business must succeed at all costs. Without the business, the family does not have much. This type of company will keep a large amount of cash in the bank *for the bad times*. This type of company will not employ too many family members, especially ones that are not productive. The company will be run very conservatively in order to stay in business and pass on to the next generation. One company I consulted with had one year's worth of income in the bank just waiting for the proverbial rainy day! Their concern was that after taking over from their father, whom they saw sacrificing and working hard, it was certainly not going to be them (the two brothers) who let down the numerous family members of the third generation the business supported.

Family Firm Financial Performance

A recent area of research that has fueled considerable discussion and debate among scholars is the superior financial performance shown by larger family firms over their nonfamily counterparts. There is conflicting research on financial performance differences between family and nonfamily firms. Recent research has shown that family businesses show a higher return on investment (Miller and Le Breton-Miller 2005), have greater value, are operated more efficiently, and carry less debt compared to nonfamily businesses (McConaughy, Matthews, and Fialko 2001). Family firms in the S&P 500 Index over the period 1992 to 2002 had higher profit margins and a higher reinvestment of revenues when compared with nonfamily firms (Lee 2006). Anderson and Reeb (2003) presented evidence showing that large family businesses in the S&P 500 Index performed better than nonfamily firms did. Miller and Le Breton-Miller wrote a book based on a yearlong study of 46 successful large family-controlled companies, including Hallmark, L. L. Bean, IKEA, the *New York Times*, SC Johnson, W. L. Gore, and Cargill (2005). The authors showed evidence that family firms outperformed their nonfamily counterparts and presented key attributes of long-term, successful family firms. Family firms have been described as "nimbler, more customer oriented and quality focused, and more active in the community. As a result, they tend to outperform nonfamily firms" (Ibrahim, Angelides, and Parsa 2008, p. 95). A study of 100 large family-owned firms by Credit Suisse showed family firms have outperformed nonfamily firms by a wide margin on numerous financial measures for the 10-year period from 2006 to 2016 (CS Family 1000, 2017).

Members from the Boston Consulting Group studied 149 publicly traded, family-controlled firms with sales of more than $1 billion. They compared results with a control group of nonfamily companies of the same size and sector, and country of origin. The results showed that during years of economic growth, the family firms did not outperform their nonfamily peers. However, during times of recession, the family-owned firms significantly outperformed nonfamily firms. When the researchers looked at data across numerous business cycles from 1997 to 2009, the average long-term financial performance of the family firms was greater than for the nonfamily firms in every country studied. The researchers speculate this was due to several factors, including family firms focusing more on resilience than performance and not maximizing their profits during positive economic times to increase their survivability during bad times. They manage the downside more than they manage the upside. The family firms were very long term in their thinking, making decisions that would be beneficial 10 to 20 years later (Kachaner, Stalk, and Bloch 2012).

Conversely, other research has presented the opposite view: that family firms are not efficient, do not manage their capital well, and have a lower return on investment. To help answer the question of whether family firms outcompete nonfamily firms, research was undertaken to find a definitive answer. The answer is: It depends. Miller and Le Breton-Miller (2011) suggest that a lone founder pursues an entrepreneurial orientation (EO) and has an advantage over second-generation family firms as the family firm has numerous social identities, loyalty, and family obligations to be concerned with, and thus underperforms due to conservatism. One study looked at 369 manufacturing businesses and found that family involvement in the management of the firm was a positive aspect and reduced its risk of failure (Revilla, Perez-Luno, and Nieto 2016). A 2015 study examined more than 350 articles on family business from 37 finance and management journals and found family business performance was moderated by succession and proper and professional corporate governance (Pindado and Requejo 2015). Investor perception on ownership concentration, and the value associated with it, is shown in a report by the Organisation for Economic Co-operation and Development (OECD). The analysis shows investors place a three percent valuation premium on firms where family insiders wield significant, but not absolute, control. Conversely, for emerging market firms where multigenerational families are majority owners, investors assign a valuation discount of 5 to 20 percent (2007).

In summary, the answer to the question of whether family firms outperform nonfamily firms or not depends on the definition of family business, which generation is in control, and if sound governance mechanisms have been employed.

Trust

A major component of the family business's competitive advantage is the high levels of trust among the family members, as well as customers, suppliers, and employees. Among family members, the trust is relational and interpersonal. Family trust is founded on connections that are much deeper than the sheer economics of the business. The foundations of trust include shared common experiences, common family characteristics, family identity and history, as well as a united value system and mutual goals. Trust is usually greater among family members than among nonfamily members and when compared with nonfamily firms. When trust is not sustained over time, conflict increases and management (agency) costs rise (Eddleston, Chrisman, Steier, and Chua 2010).

Trust plays a vital role in family firms and is a main differentiating factor between family firms and nonfamily firms. Steier (2001) proposes the role of trust as a governance mechanism in a family firm as helping to decide which governance structures to use. Building and strengthening mutual trust among the stakeholders is a critical issue for family business governance (Ward 2003).

High levels of trust have been shown to be important for consumers, suppliers, and other stakeholders as well. In a survey, family businesses were perceived as more trustworthy than nonfamily firms (75 to 59 percent). Trust of family businesses is high among the customers, suppliers, community, and employees (Edelman Trust Barometer 2017).

Problem Areas for Family Businesses

Problem areas for families in business are similar and relatively universal such as poor communication, conflict, bad decision making, failed succession, and lack of planning. Ever since Biblical times and the story of Cain and Abel, there has been interpersonal conflict, sibling rivalry, and poor communication among families. When a family comes together and forms a business unit, the same familial problems appear and can multiply. Sibling rivalry that may have started at an early age is still common and may become more pronounced in the business. In the family business, problems become more prevalent and apparent due to the family being in such close proximity with each other, and much of the family wealth is often tied up in the business. Some family members will be employed at the business and have both their wealth and livelihood intertwined in the business and with their family. Conflict can be very problematic and is common in family business (Davis and Harveston 1999; Alderson 2015). If not managed appropriately or prevented, it can derail a business and stifle growth.

To maintain family harmony, many family businesses squelch any differences of opinion, and thus suppress much of the constructive and healthy debate. It is difficult for sons and daughters to disagree with their parents, because such action is often seen as disloyal or disruptive (McCann 2007). This lack of open communication has the effect of limiting healthy discussion, potential business opportunities, as well as the entire strategic planning process. The effect is often a forced dependence upon the status quo, resulting in a lack of investment in new and emergent businesses, reduced market share, failure to recognize and respond to competitive threats, and product decline (Ward 1987).

There are numerous other situations such as poor communication, petty jealousies, entrenched CEO leadership, lack of a succession plan, nonfamily management feeling they are not respected or properly rewarded, poor decision making, problems recruiting nonfamily management, chain of command, and reporting issues (a family member reporting to another family member or to a nonfamily manager).

A global survey of 2,802 senior executives of family firms showed 43 percent of the respondents did not have a succession plan in place (PWC 2016). This is a significant problem that could result in the failure of the firm and put the family's wealth at risk. This shows once again the importance of proper governance. Creating a succession plan would be an immediate topic of discussion for any governance board or organization.

Altruism can be common in family firms (Jensen 1998) and often confounds outside advisors and other professionals. Why a firm would keep a long-term employee who was not contributing productively can be answered by the loyalty the family firm has to the employees and to the people who helped build their business. Nepotism is another problem area. It is a positive situation when a family member is promoted based on skills and experience. However, when a member of the family with little to no experience is promoted over other long-term employees (nepotism), it can cause a host of problems including a failed succession and lack of acceptance by the stakeholders, contributing to low motivation among the employees.

Drug and substance abuse issues are surprisingly common, especially among the second or third generations when money has become plentiful. If an employee had a substance abuse issue while working at a Fortune 500 firm, they would be investigated by the company's human resources department and there would be a formal corporate policy to follow. Some companies would require the employee to take a leave of absence and attempt rehabilitation, but for many companies there would be zero tolerance for this behavior and the employee would be terminated. In a family firm where the employee is also an owner, and the employee is someone's son, daughter, or brother, this issue becomes very complicated to manage. It is not easy to terminate a close family member. It causes stress among the family members and can be disruptive to the effective functioning of the company.

Triangulation

Triangulation, a common event in family firms, occurs when two warring family members bring in a third party to gain influence. As an example, a sister and a brother are at odds, and they each enlist the help of their mother to explain their viewpoints and lobby in their favor. The third party acts as a sounding board, which temporarily relieves the tension. However, continuing this type of communication is not healthy. Often, the advocacy of the triangulated person on behalf of another can make the conflict larger. The result is a problem with three people now, rather than only the original two. The best solution in this scenario is for the triangulated person to refuse to become involved and to individually counsel each family member to talk directly with the other (Rhodes and Lansky 2013). In large family businesses, multiple family members can be involved, and it can leach into entire branches of the family. Productive business is not occurring; instead, politicking is the main task at hand. At larger nonfamily companies, similar petty issues also arise, but there are policies and procedures, and a human resources department involved to help settle disputes or make recommendations for improvement.

Pruning the Family Tree

Pruning refers to family members or branches of the family being bought out by other members or branches of the family. This technique can enable a family firm to avoid conflict, possible dysfunction, and ownership dispersion by maintaining control of the business in one branch of the family. It allows inactive shareholders to turn their investments into cash and can help avoid the problem of having a multitude of owners a few generations in the future, which can cause increased conflict due to disparate goals and delayed decision making. Pruning family branches may be a possible solution to the problem of ownership imbalance. The pruning strategy is not without problems. Disagreeing over proper valuation can cause significant family conflict to the point of family members not speaking to each other. Family members who have sold may express considerable regret if the firm goes on to greater success. Due to the limited liquidity of the shares and the prohibition of selling stock to nonfamily members, this can be a ripe area for disagreement (Pearl 2010).

Generational Succession

The most problematic area for families in business is a leadership succession from one generation to the next. Many family companies fail to have a successful intergenerational succession (Ward 1986; Poza and Daugherty 2014). This can lead to a loss of family identity, wealth, legacy, and social standing in the community, and often a closure or outright sale of the business. Having effective governance structures in place enables the succession process to start and be more effective, increasing the chances of a successful succession.

CHAPTER 2

Overview of Family Business Theories

Before the reader delves into the nuts and bolts of governance, there are some theories regarding family business that need to be discussed and understood. The theories used in family business are practical and applicable. They are not what many students or business owners think of as being purely academic, not relevant, or what some feel are a waste of time. The reader needs to have a grasp of these theories because many of the governance structures work hand in hand with them. One must understand the basic theories to understand when a governance structure or mechanism does not work in a certain situation, because it is often the specific theory being used that explains its lack of effectiveness.

Agency Theory

By far one of the biggest theories when discussing governance in family business is agency (Jensen and Meckling 1976). This can be quickly explained by using the example of a real estate agent representing the sellers of a home. The real estate agent signs a contract with the sellers to represent them *as their agent* in the sale of their home. The agent compares the home with other similar homes and in consultation with the owners (who state they do not want to take less than $450,000) prices their home at $480,000 and puts it on the multiple listing service for all other real estate agents to see and advertises the home for sale. The agent is not an owner of the home, but represents the homeowners. The agent is not an employee. Suppose another couple wants to put in an offer on the home during one of the open houses held by the same agent who listed the house for sale. The couple asks the agent for the lowest price the sellers will take for the house. Instead of the usual splitting of the commission with another agent representing the buyers, this agent can "double-end it" or have what is called *dual agency*. The agent has a contract with the owners of the home, but now has an opportunity of gaining an offer from the potential buyers and will also be representing them in their purchase. In other words, the agent will earn twice as much commission! The agent is now working for both seller and buyer. What would most people do in this situation? Remember, the agent is paid on commission; he or she is not an employee and makes nothing if the house does not sell. Many people when faced with this situation and understanding they will make no money without a sale, would tell the prospective buyers, "I think they might take $450,000."

This represents what is called the *principal-agent problem*. This occurs in many human transactions, and involves what is known as self-dealing, or doing what is best for oneself. People are fallible; they are only human.

Another less harmful but nonetheless negative example suggests that an employee manager would have a reduced risk tolerance than a family owner. The manager may pass on opportunities that could benefit the business if there was risk associated with them. The manager would rather keep the status quo and have continued employment than undertake a risk that could harm their employment. Obviously, risk should be minimized, but there can be no success or growth without some risk. In family firms, each generation needs to reinvent themselves to stay current and viable in the marketplace (PWC 2016), otherwise they will lose market share to competitors or fail to respond to opportunities.

Agency theory suggests that employees may engage in self-dealing behavior if not properly supervised. The reason companies have layers of management personnel can be explained by the agency problem (type I). If employers could trust with absolute certainty that their employees would always do what is best for the business and act ethically and responsibly, the company could do with less supervisory positions and save significant labor resources.

Agency theory helps to explain one of the biggest competitive advantages a family business has over its nonfamily competitors. The company has the family unit, a loving, trusting group of people who have each other's best interest at heart. A family business can succeed with less layers of management because in the early stages of the firm the owner *is the manager*. In the next generation, the sons and daughters of the founder are in leadership, and they have become the owners. They have the same goals in mind. Family business researchers and scholars have recognized that because of this owner/manager situation, many family firms have eliminated much of the agency problem. Imagine the labor savings of not having to employ layers of supervisors and managers just to make sure the employees were acting in a responsible manner toward their employer. This can be an incredible competitive advantage for family businesses.

When family firms age and grow and advance through several generations of leadership, the family becomes more dispersed, there are fewer social ties with family members, they may have less commitment to the family business, less entrepreneurial orientation, and the agency problems once avoided with the founder/owner are now present (Eisenhardt 1989; Gomez-Mejia, Nunez-Nickel, and Guttierez 2001; Schulze et al. 2001).

Conversely, there are other sides to agency theory that are not positive, and some family business researchers use agency theory to explain a lack of competitive advantage. They have suggested ownership concentration has negative agency effects on strategy and performance as majority owners use their power to exploit the business, especially minority shareholders. This is defined as agency problem type II (Morck and Yeung 2003; Morck, Wolfenzon, and Yeung 2005).

As an example, a founder who started the firm and ran it successfully for multiple decades may decide not to retire. This is entrenched leadership, and the results can be a decline in sales and competitiveness due to the founder's unwillingness to change or adapt to new situations as they arise. This puts the organization at a competitive disadvantage and takes advantage of minority shareholders. The next generation of leaders can be frustrated with their lack of advancement and responsibility. This is one of the biggest reasons the next generation leaves the family business (Lee 2006).

Compensation can also be used as a governance tool. If the company compensates their employees and managers extremely well and provides incentive compensation opportunities, it may enable the employees to feel more like owners. They are invested in the firm's success. Now, the goals and objectives of the family and the business are aligned with those of the employees and have theoretically reduced the impact of the agency problem.

The Resource-Based View

The resource-based view (RBV; Barney 1991) of the firm states that a family firm has a set of unique capabilities, resources, and relationships that nonfamily firms do not have, and cannot develop. This may explain the competitive advantage that many family firms have over nonfamily firms (Habbershon, Williams, and MacMillan 2003). Imagine the deep relationships built by three or more generations of family members over numerous decades!

Five sources of family firm capital may help to explain the positive effects from the RBV: human capital, social capital, patient capital, survivability, and governance structures. Family business governance may be a reason why some family firms have increased performance over nonfamily firms (Habbershon and Williams 1999; Carney 2005). The advantage for a family firm comes from the interaction of the family and the business in the unique way that they manage, evaluate, acquire, discard, bundle, and leverage their resources (Chrisman, Chua, and Sharma 2003, p. 21).

The term *familiness* has been used to describe the unique and differing facets of a family business when compared with nonfamily businesses. The term is used to describe the interplay between the family and the business, including a social aspect that affects the strategic decisions of the business (Chrisman, Chua, and Steier 2005; Habbershon et al. 2003; Zellweger, Eddleston, and Kellermanns 2010).

Stewardship Theory

This approach believes the family should be caretakers of the family business. Members of families following this approach believe it is not merely theirs alone. Instead, the company is seen as an asset intended to be protected and nourished, so it can continue to provide wealth for the family and to pass down to future generations. Families utilizing this concept often hire professional outside management to run the business (Davis, Schoorman, and Donaldson 1997). These companies most commonly will have a BOD with specialized outside directors to aid in decision making and strategic planning. This approach is often seen with many of the well-known and larger publicly owned family-controlled firms seen on the Fortune 500 or the S&P 500. An example of this type of approach is the Walton family and Walmart, which uses a professional BOD and a strong management team to run their business.

Stakeholder Theory

Stakeholder theory (Freeman 1984) has recently come back into favor among the more modern progressive corporations who believe corporate social responsibility (CSR) is important and the right thing to do rather than the older and more common stockholder theory that states the sole purpose of corporations is to build wealth for stockholders (Friedman 1970). Companies utilizing the stakeholder approach believe there is more to consider than focusing all efforts on simply one stakeholder (that being the shareholder or stockholder of the firm). Instead, they believe in addition to the shareholders they also have a responsibility to employees, suppliers, customers, and the community. Stakeholder theory proposes that the needs and wants of *all* people and organizations that have a stake in the failure or success of the company should be considered. There has been an increased importance in businesses being good corporate citizens the last few decades. The general public is demanding it. The millennial generation is requiring it to be a customer of the business or an employee. This is a great competitive advantage for family-owned firms. Family business owners take pride in being respected and responsible members of the community with a reputation for fair prices and fair dealing.

As an example, a company following the stakeholder approach in a small town where they are the largest employer would consider the effect of layoffs on the economy of the town. They may still decide layoffs are needed, but at least the community, the employees, and the neighbors of the firm would be considered. It would not be purely an economic decision alone. They realize others should be considered because they would be affected by the company's decision.

Starbucks is another example of a corporation being socially responsible. The company buys its coffee beans in ways that are sustainable and promote fair trade. This means they buy only from growers who they have inspected and approved, who are growing the beans according to their specifications. Starbucks has agreed to pay a very fair price (higher than usual).

Another responsible firm, Whole Foods, promotes sustainable fisheries. These efforts cost more and make prices higher. The companies are observing the stakeholder approach and trying to be fair, or at least recognize the needs of important stakeholders. It may seem altruistic, but it is thought of as just good business. Starbucks, through their purchasing programs with small farmers, has a guaranteed supply of high-quality coffee beans. Whole Foods was reacting to its customers' concerns of overfishing and wasting nontargeted species that were caught in nets, thus protecting the fisheries for future generations. Both companies have developed a loyal base of customers who appreciate their responsible behavior.

Social Capital Theory

Effectively functioning social groups include factors such as positive interpersonal relationships, a shared sense of identity, norms, values, understanding, high trust, and cooperation. A family business with a high amount of social capital would have a tremendous competitive advantage over a nonfamily business. Social capital is one aspect of the RBV.

The Systems Approach

The systems approach is also called the three-circle model (see Figure 2.1). This is the preeminent approach to understanding family business and is now over 40 years old since its inception (Tagiuri and Davis 1996). The power of the model is its simplicity. By placing people within each circle of the model, it enables understanding of the various interrelationships and often overlapping roles of family members, owners, and employees. In an interview with John Davis, one of the creators of the approach, he admitted the model does not cover everything (such as wealth), but as a theory, it helps explain the majority of family business relationships and roles. Thus, it increases understanding of the vast complexity of the problems associated with the different constituencies, agendas, and the various people involved (FFI Practitioner 2018). It helps explain other theories such as agency, which fits into the model well. It consists of three overlapping circles. Each circle represents one of the three main subsystems of family business:

1. The family
2. The business (management)
3. Ownership

Family

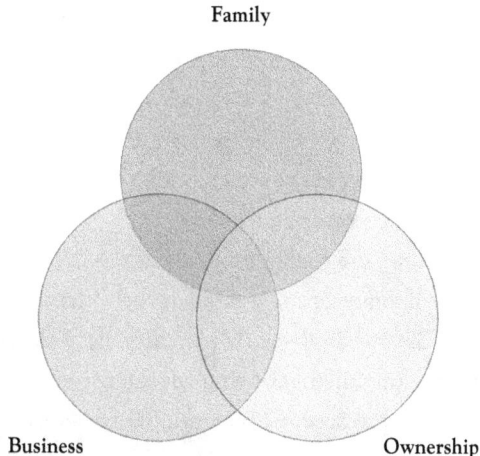

Business   Ownership

Figure 2.1 The systems approach (the three-circle model)

Source: Adapted from Tagiuri and Davis. 1996.

Understanding each subsystem in the model is critical for understanding family-owned business and their associated issues and opportunities. For example, some family members may also be employees and therefore would inhabit both the family and the business subsystems. However, if they were family members and employees, but not an owner, they would not inhabit the ownership subsystem. Sounds easy? Here is a scenario to show how helpful this model can be.

Imagine Bob, a member of a business-owning family. Bob is an employee of the company, as well as an owner. He resides in all three subsystems of the model. Because Bob works at the company, he understands the challenges and opportunities of the business at a deeper level than those who do not work there. Bob realizes the company needs to invest significant resources into new equipment to become more efficient and productive and to respond to competitive opportunities and threats.

Bob's cousin Michelle is a family member and an owner, but is not an employee. Michelle is only in two circles of the model. She does not earn income from the company as Bob does. Michelle relies on dividends due to her ownership share. During a meeting, a proposal is brought up discussing the need for the equipment and requesting the large capital expenditure. Bob is surprised when his cousin votes against the proposal! Because of Michelle and other like-minded shareholders, the equipment purchase is denied. Bob is very concerned the company may now be in jeopardy, and it will not be able to compete, thus making everyone's job harder. The cousin was concerned with her dividends that could be put into jeopardy by the large financial expenditure. Bob and his cousin have two very different priorities even though both have the same main goal of seeing the company succeed and prosper.

This example shows the usefulness of the three-circle model. Another scenario could be if one person was an owner (shareholder), but not a family member or an employee. Might they have different thoughts regarding another family member being considered for a leadership position? Might they want to accept a buyout offer rather than save the firm for future generations of family leadership? The model can explain numerous similar issues and opportunities.

Social Identity Theory

This theory looks at personal behavior as well as behavior as part of a group. It has been linked to family business studies and is the foundation for the systems approach (above) as well as the socioemotional approach (following). We all have an identity or belief of who we are, and we exhibit this as individuals and as part of a group. In the context of family business, the family has a collective identity that influences the business (Waldkirch 2015).

The Socioemotional Wealth Approach

This approach is relatively recent yet has had widespread acceptance by scholars and practitioners as a way of explaining some contrary, and some would say illogical, behavior on the part of family business owners.

The socioemotional wealth (SEW) approach discusses the belief that the business means more than just profits and dollars to the owners. The owning family receives a significant amount of noneconomic benefits by owning the business (Gomez-Mejia, Cruz, Berrone, and De Castro 2007, 2011). For example, a business-owning family from a small town may have a significant amount of social status among their neighbors and community members due to their large economic contribution to the community. The family may take great pride in the fact their grandfather started the company and the business has employed and helped hundreds, if not thousands, of people in its lifetime. The owners may gain a level of power and respect due to their ownership of the business. This SEW theory can be used to explain why a family business would decide to purchase from a supplier whose prices are higher than others, or why they would decline a buyout offer from another firm that valued the company at a very attractive price. Many families want to protect the founder's legacy. Family-owned firms have been shown to avoid making layoffs during a recession (compared with nonfamily firms) out of concern for their employees and for the family to keep its social reputation (Block 2010).

It is not all about the money! To the business-owning family, some things are more important than money. This concept is very important for suppliers, employees, customers, and the BOD to understand. It explains much of what looks to outsiders as irrational behavior on the part of the family business owners. This theory explains why some family firms are called unprofessional or poorly managed. Until one understands the real underlying goals of the family and what is important to them, they will constantly be confounded by some of the family's decisions regarding the business.

To illustrate the concept, two consultants to a large family-owned firm were shocked and surprised when they were summarily fired after recommending what they believed was a logical and rational recommendation for a layoff of employees, including family employees, who they considered too numerous and were not effectively contributing to the company. The consultants did not understand the *real* purpose of the company (to provide employment for family members) and the amount of pride and satisfaction the family felt in prospering and employing numerous people in their community.

PART II

Types of Governance for Family Businesses

CHAPTER 3

Introduction to Governance

"Family firm governance should be grounded on the unique characteristics of family firms" (Mustakillio, Autio, and Zabra 2002, p. 219). Each family is unique, and each business is unique. There is no "one size fits all" when it comes to the governance of a family business. What structure or mechanism to use is dependent upon what is needed and what is best for the family and the business. There are numerous combinations of governance mechanisms that can be used. The decision is usually made by determining what stage the business occupies, how many family members are involved, how large is the business, and its level of complexity.

This book will discuss mechanisms to:

- Separate the intertwined functions of ownership, control, and management.
- Clarify the boundaries between the family's and company's accounts.
- Develop the skills and knowledge of heirs so they can become responsible owners, so they can assume various roles as an owner, director, or employees.

Stages Where Governance Is Needed

In the startup phase of a small company with an entrepreneurial founder, the controlling owner makes most of the decisions. There are less people and employees involved in the company, no one questions their decision making, which are often made quickly and sometimes using intuition. The problems of a family business are significantly reduced or eliminated due to the low number of involved family members. The need for more formalized governance is minimal. Most governance studies assume family firms do not need formal corporate governance at the beginning of the business (Fama and Jensen 1983). However, whatever stage a firm is at, some governance is needed. It may be informal (self-governance) where a mission statement and family values predominate, or it may be more formal such as a family council or a board. The bottom line is every firm needs some type of governance (Van Aaken, Rost, and Seidl 2017).

However, as the company increases in sales and size, increases the number of employees, and increases the number of family members and generations of family members, the need for governance grows as well.

The second generation which is usually a partnership of siblings has seen the struggles of the first generation, and often worked alongside the founders to help make the business a success. They tend to have similar goals concerning the future of the business. Decisions are still relatively easy to make, there are only a few people to talk with to gather information from and gain acceptance. The need for governance is increased when the first generation begins to think about succession (turning the business over to the children). This is the first major issue that usually results in some governance structures being put into place. For example, to increase communication, family meetings that used to be an impromptu breakfast or lunch to present information to each other and make quick decisions now take on a more formal agenda. The family council may be instituted at this time as well. Decision making may only be between two sibling partners and the partners will strive for consensus (Alderson 2009, 2018).

The need for governance becomes especially important when the firm enters the third generation. This generation comes from several branches of the family, often consisting of cousins who may not know each other well or have relationships with each other. This generation can become quite large. For instance, if the original founding patriarch and matriarch have three children and each of these three siblings also has three children, there are now nine cousins involved in the third generation. If the second generation is still at the company, there are now a total of 12 people who are involved as owners, employees, or decision makers. If the first generation has not fully retired yet, it adds more complexity. In the third generation, decision making with numerous people most often happens by a majority democratic vote. This shows increased professionalism and rationality in decision making (Aronoff and Astrachan 1996). For a visual representation of the generational stages of a family business, see Figure 3.1.

Generation 1 Founder	→	Generation 2 Sibling partnership	→	Generation 3 Cousin consortium

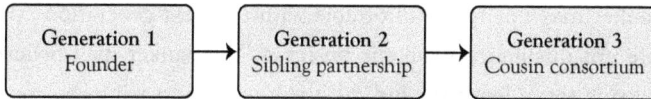

Figure 3.1 Generational stages of family business

Source: Adapted from Gersick et al. (1997).

By the second or third generation, most companies start to recognize the need and importance of governance structures and begin instituting good governance procedures to improve business productivity and effectiveness. However, some firms wait until problems appear before instituting governance practices. By then it may be too late. It has been shown that a business has a higher chance of going bankrupt due to the death or health issue of the controlling owner (who has not ceded control) than by competitive market forces (Feltham, Feltham, and Barnett 2005). Leadership succession is a process, and to be done correctly, it should be considered a long-term process. It needs to be started early, and not put off until it is too late. It is common to have a serious illness or a crisis surrounding the leader to force a company into an emergency succession that is not ideal. The company's survival is at stake.

Studies have shown the need for the next generation to be involved early and start the succession process as soon as possible. One study found that the vast majorities of decisions were made by a single individual. Usually this is the controlling owner; however, it can last well into the term of the second generation as well. This sole decision maker makes 37 percent of all decisions, and a fascinating 87 percent of all financial decisions (Feltham et al. 2005). This does not help to develop the next generation, nor properly educate and show them how to make effective decisions. It is easy to comprehend the risk and danger to the business if this sole decision maker was suddenly not there without an agreed-upon and ready successor.

This important decision maker is accustomed to a large amount of control and personal power, so it can be safe to assume the next generation has not been formally invited to meet and develop relationships with the company's vital stakeholders such as the banker, the accountant, the suppliers, or other important key customers. This is dangerous when faced with a sudden leadership succession due to a health crisis or death.

The banker may not feel comfortable with the next generation and feel they are not qualified to run the business. The banker may believe the bank's loans are in jeopardy and call them in, thus placing the company in a financial crisis as well as a leadership crisis.

Once again, the prevention of this type of adverse situation is effective family and business governance. If governance mechanisms were in place, the controlling owner would be made aware of the high risk they were assuming by their controlling actions. The succession process would have been started, and key next-generation members would already be developing relationships with important stakeholders.

However, this situation is entirely common. Most first-generation entrepreneurial founders do not look forward to stepping away from "their baby." They created the business. It is successful because of them. Their identity is tied up with the business. For many of them it is undesirable and extremely unpleasant to talk about retiring and succession. They often feel they are being "put out to pasture," and it fills them with fear and anxiety. In response, it is easier for many controlling owners to avoid the situation altogether. It is this same individual who will resist instituting proper governance, because it limits or reduces their control and power.

The Three Main Areas of Governance for Family Firms

There are three main areas of governance that affect the family business: *family governance*, *business governance*, and *governance of ownership*. Each main area will be discussed below.

Family Governance Overview

Family governance is unique to the family-owned business. It is not relevant in a nonfamily firm. There are specific mechanisms and structures put in place in a business-owning family to provide good governance for the *family*. This is separate from the more well-known business (or corporate governance) taught in university classes. Family governance mechanisms are put into place to make sure family goals are being represented separately from the business. These mechanisms include family meetings, the family council, and the constitution. Family governance concerns itself with:

- The family's involvement and participation in the business
- The role and image of the family (and thus the business) in the community
- Providing and ensuring effective family communication
- Enabling transparency in business operations
- Providing information and education regarding the business
- Continuity of the family's shared interest in the business
- The continued health and prosperity of the business
- Ensuring the continuation of family values and goals
- Protecting the legacy of the founder/s
- Adhering to the mission of the family
- Interacting with the BOD and presenting the family's viewpoint to the board

Business Governance Overview

Business governance (commonly known as corporate governance), involves the structures put into place to help the business be more professional, make better decisions, communicate more effectively, and are the major concerns of management. The chief executive officer and TMT are responsible for the effective running of the business. In a first-generation founder-led business, the founder will perform many of these roles. In a third-generation business, the business is larger, more complex, and more professional with significantly more governance mechanisms such as a BOD to oversee effective management and productive running of the business. Business governance concerns itself with day-to-day operations and management of the business, such as:

- Finance
- Operations
- Supplier relationships

- Customer relationships
- Employees, human resources
- Ensuring the appropriate organizational structure for maximum effectiveness
- The TMT
- The BOD

Governance of Ownership Overview

The ownership group needs effective governance as well. The shareholders council and the shareholders annual meeting are the two governance tools associated with ownership. The main responsibility is overseeing the BOD. This aspect of governance concerns itself with the ownership of the business and the issues and responsibilities associated with being a shareholder:

- Overseeing the BOD
- Recruitment and selection of new directors
- Succession to the next generation of leadership
- Financial performance
- Providing effective liquidity
- Deciding on the strategic direction of the firm
- Protecting the investment of the shareholders
- Allocating capital

Tables 3.1 and 3.2 provide readers with a graphical overview of who (family, ownership, and business) is responsible for using the governance mechanisms, the variety of issues covered in governance, and at what stage each mechanism is usually used.

Table 3.3 identifies the proper governance tools or mechanisms commonly employed for each stage of the family business.

Each of the three major areas of governance for family firms will be discussed in detail in the next chapters.

Table 3.1 Governance responsibilities

Governance Issues	Family	Ownership	The Business (Management)
Family Mission/Vision/Values	1		
Setting Family Policy	1		
Family Members' Personal Relations	1		
Family Communication	1		
Preventing/Resolving Family Conflict	1		
Family Employment	1		
Aiding Family	1		
Charity/Philanthropy	1		
Protection of Family Legacy/Social Status	1		
Community Relations	2		1
Education	1		
Protection of Family Brand	2		1
Strategy	2	2	1
Review Business Performance	2	1	2
Daily Operations			1
Employee Relations	2		1
Compensation	2		1
Succession	1	2	2
Family and Business Interactions	1		1
Board Makeup	1	1	2
Selection of Board Members	2	2	1
Election of Board Members	2	1	2
Ethics	2	2	1
Corporate Culture	2		1
Dividends	2	2	1
Supplier and Customer Relations			1
Liquidity	2	1	2
Valuation and Market for Shares		1	
Capital Allocation	2	1	1

Primary responsibility = 1; Secondary responsibility = 2.

Table 3.2 Primary responsibility for governance mechanisms

Governance Tools	Family	Ownership	The Business (Management)
The Mission/Vision/Values	1		2
Family Meetings/Retreats	1		
Family Council	1		
Family Constitution	1		
Board of Advisors	1		
BOD	2		1
Compensation	2		1
Philanthropy	1		2
Shareholder Meetings		1	
Shareholder Annual Meeting		1	2
Family Office	1		

Primary responsibility = 1; Secondary responsibility = 2.

Table 3.3 Stages where governance mechanisms are needed

Stage of Company	Governance Mechanisms Employed
Founder/Entrepreneur (Generation One)	(Informal) Family Meetings
Generation Two A Partnership of Siblings	(More formal) Family Council Creation of a Board of Advisors
Generation Three A Larger Group of Cousins	(Formal) Family Council Family Constitution Shareholder Committee BOD Annual General Meeting (AGM)

CHAPTER 4

Family Governance

Mission/Vision

A vitally important aspect of family business uniqueness yet one that is often overlooked is the creation of a mission statement. For many businesses, the mission is often profit maximization or market dominance. Family-owned businesses often have a mission or purpose that is different than other companies. For many families the goal is to build their wealth in the first and second generations of family leadership. Many firms change their goals to one of stewardship that passes it on to future generations, protecting their social standing in the community and protecting their family legacy.

To enable the future success of the firm, a mission statement is vital to show all stakeholders what the purpose of the firm is and what it stands for. A strong well-crafted mission statement can be used as a decision-making tool when a decision is hard to make. If the mission is front and center to the operation of the business, a member just needs to ask, "Does the decision I am making fit with our mission?" If the answer is negative, it is an easy decision to make. A good practice in family business governance is to have two mission statements: one for the family and a separate mission statement for the firm. The mission statement would be created at a family council meeting and then put forth for ratification by all family members at an annual meeting.

Example of a Family Mission Statement

The Smith family is a group of entrepreneurial family members in business together. Our purpose is to successfully grow and develop as a family through our business interests. Our family and our businesses are both important; they are intertwined. Success in the family leads to success in business. We strive to maintain family harmony, respect, love, and togetherness as we do business together. We agree to work hard to help every family member achieve their goals. We will support and invest in new ventures to enable our family to higher levels of success.

Values

Another major difference between family firms and nonfamily firms are the values of the family and the business. As the business and the family are intertwined, the values of the family guide decision making and are paramount in the business. The family name is often on the front door and the family feels an extra responsibility to act in a way that represents their family in a positive light. Aligning family values with the business values is an important guiding principle that many family firms hold dear (Table 4.1).

Table 4.1 Common values associated with successful family firms

Integrity	Good Work Ethic
Honesty	Trust
Truthfulness	Open Communication
Stewardship	Long-Term View
Protect the Legacy	Personal Growth
Value and Respect for Family and Employees	Create Value for the Business
Dedication	

Large Family-Owned/Family-Controlled Corporate Mission/Vision/Values/Purpose Statements

The following are examples of statements from family firms:

SC Johnson
SC Johnson has a four-page document entitled *This We Believe* that details the values and the guiding principles of the family and the company. These principles were first summarized in 1927 by H.F. Johnson, Sr.

The goodwill of people is the only enduring thing in any business. It is the sole substance . . . the rest is shadow!

The company strives to serve and earn the trust of the following five groups of people:

- Employees. We believe that the fundamental vitality and strength of our worldwide company lies in our people.
- Consumers and Users. We believe in earning the enduring goodwill of consumers and users of our products and services.
- General Public. We believe in being a responsible leader within the free market economy.
- Neighbors and Hosts. We believe in contributing to the well-being of the countries and communities where we conduct business.
- World Community. We believe in improving international understanding (SCJohnson.com n.d.-a)

Chick-fil-A
Chick-fil-A does not have a mission statement; instead, they have a corporate purpose:

To glorify God by being a faithful steward of all that is entrusted to us. To have a positive influence on all who come in contact with Chick-fil-A (Chick-fil-A.com). It is easy to see how this purpose reflects the Christian values of the company founder, S. Truett Cathy and his family.

Bacardi Limited
Family-owned Bacardi Limited has the three pillars of:

Fearless, Family, and Founders. The pillars stand for our belief that being fearless means being empowered to challenge the norm and innovate; as a family company we will take care of each other and our communities; and our employees will act with a founder's mentality, always doing what is right and taking accountability to ensure the sustainability of our company. (BacardiLimited.com 2018)

Hallmark Cards

Founded in 1910 and still led by family, privately held Hallmark Cards Inc. states their vision and values below. Notice their desire to benefit their local community as well as stay privately held.

Our Vision

> We will be the company that creates a more emotionally connected world by making a genuine difference in every life, every day.

We Believe

> That our products and services must enrich people's lives.
>
> That creativity and quality—in our products, services, and all that we do—are essential to our success.
>
> That innovation in all areas of our business is essential to attaining and sustaining leadership.
>
> That the people of Hallmark are our company's most valuable resource.
>
> That distinguished financial performance is imperative to accomplish our broader purpose.
>
> That our private ownership must be preserved.

We Value

> Excellence in all we do.
>
> High standards of ethics and integrity.
>
> Caring and responsible corporate citizenship for Kansas City and for each community in which we operate.
>
> These beliefs and values guide our business strategies, our corporate behavior, and our relationships with business partners, suppliers, customers, communities, and each other (Hallmark.com).

Example of a Family Business Mission Statement

The Smith Corporation is in its third generation of family leadership. Our founder Thomas Smith created our company based on three values:

- Supply excellent high-quality products to our stakeholders at fair prices.
- Engage all of our stakeholders with integrity, truthfulness, and honesty.
- Provide our employees with good jobs that provide a living wage and potential for advancement.

We will never forget who made us successful. The Smith family donates five percent of all net profits to local charities in the community.

Goals and Objectives

Families in business together also have different goals and objectives than nonfamily firms. The goal of one family may be continued family leadership throughout the generations. Another may desire to have their children go into whatever career they would like in order to fulfill their potential and the business is designed to support them. Another family may be entrepreneurial and use their business as a family bank to support family members and start new organizations that benefit family members. All families are unique, they put their imprint on the business with their mission, vision, values, and goals and objectives.

Family Meetings

The first and simplest mechanism of family governance is having family meetings. These happen informally in the early years of the firm. Family meetings are the key to effective communication at this stage. They can be as simple as an informal breakfast or lunch to discuss business issues and opportunities, and to keep everyone updated. In the later years as a company grows and has a larger number of employees and family shareholders, the need for more effective communication increases. In the second and third generations and beyond, there are other governance structures such as the shareholder council and the family council that will take on more importance. The purpose of a family meeting is to increase communication and make sure everyone has the chance to hear the same current information (not secondhand), and to have the ability to share their own points of view and ask questions. In this manner, everyone is on the same page, attendees feel respected by being allowed to present opinions and concerns, and the family can discuss areas of importance for each member.

Who should attend family meetings? There is no universal answer for this question. The best answer is, it depends on the type of family, the personalities involved, and the individual business. Some family business consultants recommend only family owners and family employees attend the meetings. Others recommend that spouses and in-laws attend the meetings to better understand what is happening, as their lives are also affected by what happens in the firm. As an example, if a family meeting were held without spouses and the company needed to have a round of pay cuts, a nonemployed spouse would appreciate much more information as to the reason and the necessity. By attending the meetings, they would be provided with the information firsthand and would have better understanding and potentially buy into the decision at a greater level. Without good information, they may disagree, decide it is not needed, spread dissent, and create conflict.

Family owners/employees are used to having very informal family meetings spontaneously such as a quick lunch. When the professionalism of the family meetings is increased, the attendees need to be the same regular attending members. There are other governance mechanisms that can provide increased communication for other members of the family and will be discussed later.

Family Retreats and Holidays

Family retreats are designed to keep the entire family close and to celebrate accomplishments and achievements of family members. In the third generation and after, families can become quite large. One southern California family-owned automotive dealership had annual family retreats consisting of over 150 people. Especially in larger families, but in smaller ones as well, people can lose track of what is going on in other family members' lives. The retreat is an attempt to keep the family engaged and engender family love and trust. In a retreat, everyone is invited, children as well. Some families accomplish this by going away to a cabin in the woods or a beach resort on a semiannual basis, others do it once a year and use it as a minivacation for family members. Some families use some of their financial capital and buy a condominium in Hawaii, or a home on a lake for the dual purposes of family personal use and a place to gather as a family for retreats. The retreat has a loose agenda, there are a few days of fun and family activities, mixed with some business meetings, and often presentations by family business professionals such as life insurance agents, estate planners, and consultants on topics such as improving communication, financial planning, succession, or improving decision making. Competitions and games are used to build teamwork among family members.

Through retreats, children of family business owners get introduced to the purpose of the business, and to its mission and vision at an early age. They see the importance of the business to their family and learn family history passed down from multiple generations. The purpose of inviting the children is to make them knowledgeable concerning the business and shape their view of the business. The task is for them to see it as a legacy and something valuable, and not as a negative that takes too much of mom and dad's time.

A sample agenda for a family retreat is as follows:

8:00 a.m.	Breakfast and socializing
9:00 a.m.	Welcome and discussion of agenda
9:10 a.m.	Family updates
10:00 a.m.	Progress report by the CEO
10:30 a.m.	Family philanthropy discussion
11:00 a.m.	Presentation by Estate Planning Professional/Life Insurance Professional
12:00 noon	Lunch (Children welcome for the rest of the afternoon)
1:30 p.m.	History of the business, history of the founders
2:30 p.m.	Generational meeting breakout sessions
3:30 p.m.	Discussion of breakout sessions
4:00 p.m.	Fun activity

Generational Meetings

Specific generational meetings are useful to increase communication with fellow members of the same generation. It is easy to see how a member of the second generation may have the same issues as other second-generation members. Family business consultants and university-based family business centers provide workshops for each generation, dividing the participants into specific cohort groups which accomplishes two important roles. First, participants are freely able to discuss their issues in a safe environment, free from disagreement or criticism by a family member from a different generation. Second, other members of the same generation can usually relate to the issue, since they are more than likely experiencing a similar issue. The cohort group members realize they are not alone, and that others may feel similarly.

Consultants will often use this approach to start a family retreat. They will separate the various generations into their own specific meetings, and then bring the family back together to discuss the issues. It is interesting to see the differences in the various generations. For example, the second generation may have differing opinions concerning times they have tried to take more responsibility only to get countermanded by members of the first generation. The first generation often complains the second generation does not step up and take responsibility enough!

Family Assembly

There are many names families use to describe some governance mechanisms. Some families have a family assembly. This assembly is for the entire family including spouses and children. This organization is not focused on decision making. Instead, its focus is to nurture the family, to create tight bonds with each other, to make sure the family is healthy, and to ensure all family members feel a sense of togetherness (Eckrich and McClure 2012). The family retreats and holidays would be a part of the family assembly.

Family Philanthropy

Many families in business together use philanthropy as a way of binding the family closer together. Once businesses reach a certain level of success, many of them will donate a certain percentage of their profits to charities or causes that are important to the family. Research shows the vast majority of family corporate giving is to their own local community as a way of paying back the people who enabled their success. Education, children, and then religious giving follow (Breeze 2009).

The philanthropic arm of the organization can be a useful avenue for many nonemployed family members. This keeps them engaged with the family and the business and provides satisfaction regarding their family benefiting society. As an example, Trudy Cathy White is the sister of current Chick-fil-A President Dan Cathy. She is not employed at the family-owned corporation as her two brothers are. She stayed engaged by being involved in the WinShape Foundation, the charitable arm of the Chick-fil-A family. It focuses on education, provides young people tuition for summer camps, and benefits foster children. All are causes important to their father and founder of the company S. Truett Cathy. They honor his legacy with their charitable giving.

The Family Constitution

The constitution is one of the most vital tools for families in the governance area. In the United States it is called the constitution. In other areas such as Europe, or Latin and South America it is referred to as a protocol. Some call it a family agreement or charter.

The constitution is a written document. It is a living document that can be updated and changed as needed. This important document puts into writing what the family has agreed upon concerning the business. Writing the constitution is an exhaustive process. and it takes a significant amount of time to finish. It is commonly worked on during family meetings and family retreats, and it is not uncommon for it to take years to complete. Depending on the size of the company, some families have the family council compose the first draft and then present it to the entire family for suggestions and recommendations.

The family constitution has multiple purposes. One large benefit of the constitution is to bring up important and often problematic areas in advance and before they actually happen. These areas could devolve in the future into business disruption and/or interpersonal conflict. Writing the constitution allows family members to discuss the issues and what should be done to prevent, eliminate, or manage them. Another benefit of the constitution is for the family to document *in writing* important procedures of how family business items will be addressed, and it can be used similarly as a policies and procedures manual. This document is vital to the professionalism and effective management of the firm (Montemerlo and Ward 2011).

The constitution gains its power and authority because all the decision makers have input into what goes into the constitution. The family members discuss and write the constitution together. There is consensus, there is agreement and buy in because all family members were allowed input. The family members agree to abide by the guidelines and procedures spelled out in the constitution. This is a vital area of importance. Once decisions are made, the family needs to have unity and agreement without complaining members of the family spreading dissent to employees or management. There is power in numbers and unification.

The Vital Importance of the Constitution in Preventing Conflict and Dysfunction

The importance of the family constitution can best be understood by some examples: A young son of a business-owning family is hired after attending college. After a few years he is promoted to a supervisory position. The son has a harsh management style and begins to treat employees in an abusive manner. A female employee accuses the son of harassment and sues the company after reporting the situation to family members (since there was no human resources department), and no action was made to resolve the incident or investigate it. Several other employees claim similar treatment. The business is facing serious liability. Several family members of different branches of the family want to terminate the offending employee. It is easy to see the mom or dad of the offending family member wanting to protect their child and disagreeing with other family members. This type of situation is loaded with conflict and can devolve into serious interfamily dysfunction.

If the family had a written constitution and discussed this type of event in advance, the decision concerning what to do about the family employee would have already been made. It would have been made previously, and at a time when emotions were not running high. All the family members would have agreed to abide by it. The constitution will limit the amount of disagreement and conflict.

In another family firm, a daughter marries a young man whom the family does not approve. The daughter failed to obtain a prenuptial agreement with her husband. It is not a healthy relationship. Eventually, they divorce, the former husband sues for half of the daughter's ownership shares in the company. The family members are aghast at the possibility of being "partners" with the former husband. This is the type of issue that is commonplace and needs to be discussed in advance to be prevented. If the family had decided on a shareholder policy prohibiting nonfamily ownership, and what to do in the case of a family member's divorce, such as requiring prenuptial agreements, or establishing a buyout fund to purchase family members' shares, the problem could have been prevented or eliminated.

What the Constitution Covers

The mission and vision of the organization are paramount and are placed at the top of the constitution. The purpose of the organization is important to communicate to younger generations. Every decision is seen through the "lens" of the mission and vision of the organization. Often, family members will ask themselves "what would grandpa do?" Or "what would mom do in this situation?" Having the mission and vision at the top of the document shows the family members what their company stands for (and most importantly what it will not stand for) and details the company's lasting and important values.

The constitution covers a multitude of possibilities. It is obviously impossible to cover every contingency, but the constitutions being written today have benefited from 20 years of trial and error by previous family-owned businesses and by family business consultants. In a nutshell, the constitution covers employment issues; what the process is for entering the business (college degree, previous experience working at another firm); stock valuation; the mission, vision, and purpose of the company (is it to pass on to future generations, or to sell?); shareholder ownership policies; termination and hiring policies; who reports to who; buyout agreements; compensation for family and nonfamily; what the process is for leaving the firm; etc.

Suggested Outline/Questions for the Creation of a Family Constitution

The following is a list of questions for families to ask of themselves, discuss, find agreement, and then document into their written family constitution. It is not an exhaustive list, it covers many of the most important items. At a minimum, it can be used to spur families as to the types of questions to discuss. If the family uses a facilitator in the form of a family business consultant, they will have lists of questions they feel are important and have been shown to speed up the process of writing a constitution:

> What is the policy for a family member to enter the business?
> Is there a certain number of family members allowed into the business?
> What is the procedure for terminating an employed family member?
> Who can own shares in the business?
> Should shareholders be restricted to family members?
> What are the rates of compensation for family members? Nonfamily members?
> What positions are nonfamily members able to hold?
> What is the process for succession (choosing the next leader)? Will it be limited to family members?
> What must a potential successor have done/accomplished before being considered?
> How should a successor development plan be developed?
> What are the requirements for a family employee to be promoted?
> To whom should family members report? Should they be required to report to nonfamily members?
> What is the process for how decisions are to be made?
> How many members should sit on the family council?
> Who should be invited to family business meetings?
> Should the family council member's terms rotate?

How shall the shareholder committee operate?

How many members will make up the shareholder committee?

How will a BOD or advisors be nominated?

Should the chair of the board also be the chief executive officer (dual role)?

How many outside directors should sit on the BOD?

How many inside directors should sit on the BOD?

What is the policy for family employees who have a substance abuse problem?

What is the policy for family members guilty of a crime?

What is the policy for harassment in the workplace?

How should the family, the business, and ownership be governed?

What is the process for buying back shares?

How will shares be valued?

How will retirement be handled upon a successful succession of leadership?

How should interpersonal conflict be dealt with among family members?

The Family Council

The family council has often been used in place of the shareholders council and the BOD in smaller firms. The creation of a family council and moving to a democratic majority vote decision-making process is often one of the first recommendations made by family business consultants. In older and larger firms with more family members, the council is more formalized. Members are voted onto the council at the yearly shareholders meeting, and decisions are made by voting and presented to the larger shareholder council for ratification.

Responsibilities of the Family Council

One of the biggest responsibilities of the family council is the drafting and creation of the family constitution. The council can make initial drafts based on family input and then present the proposed document at the annual shareholders meeting for ratification. The process is long and rigorous, but the benefit for the family can be immeasurable in preventing conflict and disagreement, and for continuation of the family's mission and values throughout the generations. The mission and values should be incorporated into every decision the family council makes.

Another large responsibility of the family council is electing from its membership one- or two-family council representatives to present the views of the family to the BOD. The directors give time during each board meeting (it is on the agenda) to listen to the views of the family and will then have knowledge concerning the family's views on certain situations and areas of importance. Considering the SEW concept, the board is often not aware of what the family may value. It can very often be counterintuitive. The board may arrive at what they consider to be an excellent strategy; however, if it goes against the wishes of the family, there will be problems. By having a member of the family council sit on the BOD as the family representative, the board is made aware of the thoughts, feelings, and concerns of the family on important issues that affect the family. For example, the board may not realize the deep-natured feelings the owners have to protect the founder's legacy. Or, the value of the social status family members have merely by being an owner of the firm. The family would want their thoughts known regarding anything having to do with respect to the family legacy or anything that could impact their social standing in the community (Eckrich and McClure 2012).

Structure of the Family Council

The structure of the council is formalized. Its meetings are scheduled far in advance, it has a written agenda. Often, it is facilitated by a family business consultant who is charged with keeping the meeting on track. This is an important task when the business is in the early stages of family council formation. The controlling owner may tend to dominate the meeting, which has the effect of hampering discussion and opposing views. The facilitator is experienced in politely facilitating a meeting where everyone has a say, and the controlling owner is now a member and not the sole vote or decision maker. Decisions are now made democratically, by voting. In smaller firms, all shareholders are usually members. In larger firms, the council is limited to those members who have been elected by the shareholder council, usually at the annual meeting. At inception, the number of family members on the council is relatively small. As the company grows, numerous family members may want to be involved. The family must now decide who should be on the board by a democratic vote at the annual shareholder meeting.

A family council should have a budget to pay for travel costs of family members, trips for continuing education or conferences, honorarium, and to reimburse members for attending family events associated with the business, such as a family meeting or a family retreat.

Interaction with the Board

In the early days of the firm, the family council will function as the BOD. As the company grows and enters the mid-second-generation and third-generation stages, the addition of a BOD is prudent. The family council will elect one member to serve on the BOD and will communicate the desires of the family to the board.

Family Business Checklist

The following are helpful questions for family councils to consider and discuss. These questions are helpful when developing the family constitution and when considering succession:

1. Do we have a valid business plan?
2. Do we have a clear and agreed-upon mission statement for the family as well as the business?
3. Are our company values clear?
4. Do we have a vision for the future of our company?
5. Do we have a strategic plan for the business?
6. Do we have a family business constitution?
7. How will we make decisions? Who will make decisions?
8. Does the business have specific sales and profit goals?
9. Are the family business goals agreed on by the family?
10. How do family members feel about selling the business outside of the family?
11. Should we work with consultants? Under what circumstances?
12. Is there a fair compensation and reward system for family as well as nonfamily members?

13. Is the compensation system based on market value?
14. Is there an employee performance appraisal system?
15. Who should evaluate family employees?
16. Do we have nonfamily managers, and do we encourage them?
17. What are the rights and responsibilities of nonfamily employees?
18. Are there policies for family members to join or exit the business?
19. Should the next generation be required to obtain a university education before entry into the firm?
20. Should the next generation be required to have some outside work experience before entry into the firm? If so, how much?
21. Do we have written hiring and firing policies and procedures?
22. Do we have written job descriptions?
23. Should a board of advisors or directors be instituted?
24. Should we start a family council?
25. Is there a succession plan?
26. Is a system for successor development in place?
27. Is there a process in place for choosing a successor?
28. Are there structures in place to increase family communication?
29. Is there a significant amount of interpersonal conflict? Sibling rivalry?
30. Is there a conflict management and resolution system?
31. How does the family feel about selling shares to the public?
32. What role does debt play in the firm? How much or how little?
33. How much risk do we feel comfortable having?
34. Is the next generation interested in the business?
35. Are all family members welcome to join the firm?
36. Are our sales increasing? Is the industry highly competitive?
37. Is the industry outlook positive?
38. Is the business financially healthy?
39. Are women treated equally in the business?

Questions for the Next Generation

1. Is it your intention to enter the family firm?
2. Why do you want to join the firm?
3. Do you have necessary experience and education?
4. What are your strengths and skills that can aid the company?

5. Are you willing to make sacrifices for the firm, such as receiving low pay or working long hours when necessary?
6. What is your long-term vision for the company?
7. Are your values in line with the founder's values and the company's stated mission?
8. Have you gained any outside work experience?
9. Do you feel pressured to be the successor? Is it your choice?
10. Do you believe the business should stay in the family?

There are numerous questions, and these would require a significant amount of time and attention to answer. The families who have successfully managed intergenerational successions and moved to more professional levels of management have successfully worked through many of these questions.

Board of Advisors

Instituting a board of advisors is another positive step to increase the professionalism of a family-owned firm. When a privately held family firm grows, it lessens its dependence on the original controlling owner as it enters its second and third generations. Having a board of advisors as a sounding board and to provide recommendations and advice can be very beneficial. Family members grew up in the same house, they speak the same language, and use the same terminology. They tend to have related views and think similarly to each other. The board of advisors provides different views and perspectives that the family has often not considered.

Ideally, this board should be made up of successful businesspeople in the local community that the owners respect. It should not have the company accountant or the company attorney as a member. The board is stronger with more outside views that are independent from those of the owner or the company. Another accountant, a different banker, and a different attorney should sit on the board of advisors to allow the family to benefit from different advice and views. The purpose of the board of advisors is to obtain many different perspectives, and be presented with different voices, views, and experiences, than those of the insiders in the business.

The board of advisors should be considered informal and advisory only. The board's recommendations, although valuable, do not have formal authority as those of a BOD. The business is under no obligation to accept or act on the recommendations put forth by the board. Many advisory boards are voluntary; recently, family-owned companies have begun compensating board members for their time and service with an honorarium or a stipend per meeting. Many advisory boards meet annually or twice yearly. The owners can make phone calls between meetings to obtain advice from their members as well; this is a very common use of the advisors. It can be tremendously beneficial for an owner to solicit advice when making a large decision. The advisory board is also a step in the direction of a BOD once the company grows.

Estate Planning

It is not the purpose of this book to make any recommendations for estate and tax planning purposes. Professionals (tax attorneys, accountants, and estate planners) should be consulted. The rules and guidelines often change. This subject matter is vitally important; the success or failure of the business rides on effective estate planning for future generations to thrive. This is a vital area to be discussed using the various governance structures the family and the business have. Many families are often unaware of the costs involved to successfully navigate a transition of leadership from one generation to the next. Costs that are often overlooked include fees for certified public accountants, attorneys, insurance, taxes, and costs for professional advisors. The need for an up-to-date and realistic business valuation is critical.

Family business owners often want to divide the ownership shares of the business equally among all the children. However, equal ownership can be problematic when inactive shareholders have an equal vote with active (employed) shareholders. If an outside shareholder's concern is for income/dividend maximization, the individual may often vote against capital expenditures needed for growth, diversification, or equipment purchases. This handcuffs the TMT and the family to effectively operate the business.

If the firm shares were split equally with the second generation, by the third generation imbalances in share count can occur, with larger families having significantly dispersed and divided ownership. This gives them a smaller share of ownership per family member. A childless heir would have a significantly larger percentage of share ownership and thus control. This is setting up the family for a potential conflict with this type of imbalanced share distribution. Certain branches of the family would be significantly more powerful than others, simply due to good intentions of fairness by the previous generations.

Nonvoting Stock

One of the techniques estate planners suggest in succession planning with family firms is the creation of nonvoting stock. Inactive family members can be owners of the firm, but not decision makers in the firm. The technique has negative aspects associated with it as well, especially when a new generation of descendants of inactive family members becomes active in the family firm. Again, the family business should consult specialized professionals such as an attorney.

CHAPTER 5

Governance of the Business

The Board of Directors

In the United States, officers of the corporation must be elected, and an annual meeting with recorded notes is required. It is a requirement to establish a board of directors (BOD) when creating a new corporation. The directors have the responsibility and authority of providing effective oversight of the corporation. They have the obligation and responsibility to hire and terminate the CEO and the TMT. The purpose of the board is to provide a system of checks and balances to ensure oversight, help provide accountability, and make recommendations to the TMT. A BOD is not like a board of advisors who merely provide advice, when the BOD makes recommendations, the management must comply.

Smaller family firms often do not utilize a BOD, instead opting for the founder and spouse in the early days to be the "board" (informal governance), and in later years the family council serves this purpose.

Suggested Sample of Board of Directors' (BOD) Objectives

1. To be an entity elected by the company shareholders to which the officers of the company are accountable, as well as to provide a forum for shareholders, officers, employees, and creditors, ensuring that the company assets are valid as reported.
2. To assist in the strategic planning process.
3. To ask tough, challenging questions, offer a fresh perspective to management, and hold the CEO and management of the company accountable for results.

4. To provide help, leadership, support, advice, and experience to the officers of the company and to approve of their actions to achieve profitable growth.
5. To always be learning about the company and the industry. This might include visiting customers and vendors and possibly attending industry association meetings.
6. To continually review corporate goals, and objectives and policies. To serve on committees as needed.
7. To take responsibility for making sure that the company follows all SEC, and local, state, and federal requirements.
8. To aid the organization by using their own social networks and experience.
9. To assist the shareholders with the succession planning process.
10. To recommend future board members.

A primary responsibility of the BOD is to consider the business *separately* from the needs of the family. The needs of the family are to be discussed in the family council. The family council representatives make recommendations to the BOD on behalf of the family.

Awareness of proper and effective corporate governance has been on the increase in many countries around the world. Because of ethical lapses of companies such as Tyco, WorldCom, and Enron, as well as Arthur Andersen, governments and regulating bodies have increased governance guidelines and expectations for corporations. Since the Great Recession, the pressure on corporations to be good corporate citizens and to act in a responsible manner has increased, not just in the United States, but internationally as well. There has been an increased focus on the stakeholders of a firm, transparency, independent directors, and accountability. Good corporate governance can help accomplish these goals. Investors are also demanding increased governance. A survey of investors showed that they value good governance as being on par with financial considerations when evaluating investments. Investors have also been shown to pay a premium for investing into a firm with high standards of governance (McKinsey & Company 2002).

In the United States, stock market changes and SEC changes tightened and increased corporate governance requirements. The Sarbanes–Oxley

Financial Accountability Act (Sarbox) was put into place in 2002 in response to the failings and ethical misdeeds of companies in the 1990s. This act concerns itself primarily with public companies; however, many banks and other stakeholders are requiring that privately held firms align themselves with Sarbox as well. A major concern of Sarbox was that many BODs were found to be overweight with insiders and friends of the CEO. In family firms especially, the boards mainly consisted of insiders and family members who would be loyal to the family leader. Because of the revised regulations, boards are now required to have a balance between inside directors, outside directors, and management.

Boards now have a legal responsibility to oversee the business, and not just to rubberstamp the desires of the CEO. Board members have professional liability if they do not act with the best intentions for the stockholders. Company officers now must sign their name on the financial statements stating as to there their accuracy, and not mislead stockholders. The penalty for failure can be severe, up to incarceration. Penalties for fraud and bribery were increased. Another major emphasis was to make sure companies treated all shareholders equally, including minority (small) shareholders. This has had a huge impact on publicly owned family firms, which commonly made decisions that benefited only the family. As an example of the newer regulations, Robert Mondavi Corporation was forced to sell his family-owned wine company even though he had a significant majority of the stock. The minority shareholders were appalled, became very vocal, and threatened a lawsuit when the firm did not accept an overly generous buyout offer from Constellation Brands. Robert Mondavi did not want to sell the firm that he started, but wanted to pass it on to his son (Siler 2007). The regulations stated that all shareholders (including minor shareholders) needed to be treated with fairness. This should be a cautionary tale to family firms considering going public.

Instituting a BOD is a major area of opportunity for many family firms to improve their corporate governance and company performance. Research has shown that improved decision making occurs in family firms with strong, active boards (Mustakallio & Autio 2001; Mustakallio, Autio, and Zahra 2002; Ward 1988). Research has shown that the contribution of effective BODs made firms less likely to go out of business and they exhibited increased performance compared with their peers (Brenes, Madrigal, and Requena 2009; Wilson, Wright, and Scholes 2017).

Family businesses with strong BODs have been shown to be more effective and have improved decision-making ability (Eddleston, Otondo, and Kellermanns 2008). The research is clear on this point. This is partially due to the beneficial aspects of conflict. Not all conflict is bad; there are also positive forms of conflict such as work-task conflict where there is a healthy debate regarding the best way to do the work. This leads to better decision making (Kellermanns and Eddleston 2004; Eisenhardt, Kahwajy, and Bourgeois 1997; Eddleston and Kellermanns 2007). Diversity of opinion and good debate lead to directors having open communication concerning issues of importance. At board meetings now, viewpoints are presented that normally would have been muted in the past by the amount of insider's present. By discussing a variety of ideas and solutions to problems, family businesses make better decisions (Aronoff and Astrachan 1996).

Research shows that the more frequently the board meets, the better its performance. Twelve meetings a year is best with four meetings a year the new minimum. Increased board-meeting frequency leads to better knowledge of the business in the case of nonfamily board members, as well as increased commitment and participation (Brenes, Madrigal, and Requina 2009). The vast majority of firms who have a BOD rate its contribution as good to excellent (MassMutual 2002). An updated PWC study shows an increase in the number of family firms utilizing BODs over the last decade. In a survey of 147 family-owned and owner-operated firms, 59 percent reported having a formal BOD (PWC 2014).

To create good debate and foster constructive and positive conflict, the board must have nonfamily members serving on it, as well as people from outside the firm. The usefulness of a BOD, whose membership consists of those with significant experience outside the family and the business, is especially apparent when the firm is run by a charismatic and very powerfully assertive founder or other family member. A broader range of ideas, suggestions, and recommendations can now be discussed, especially those not previously seen as favorable by the family member in control. It is easy to comprehend the difficulty of voting against a father or other relative, especially if this relative is in a senior position. When income, wealth, and future employment are intertwined, having full communication with powerful family members can be difficult.

Research shows that BODs that are balanced between insiders and outsiders enhance company management by adding objectivity. Having nonfamily board members was seen as enabling confidence and trust for family members not active at the firm. Results show that contributions from both family and nonfamily directors complement each other. Family board members have valued experience and knowledge of their business. Conversely, nonfamily board members provide objective vision and a more professional viewpoint. Nonfamily board members often act as arbitrators to help solve conflict in the business and within the family. This provides family members with valued objectivity, which can only be provided by someone outside the family. This helps to prevent resentment and the risk of poor family unity (Brenes et al. 2009).

Herschend Family Entertainment is the largest family-owned entertainment company in the United States with over 10,000 employees spread over six states. It has been family-owned and operated since its inception (http://www.hfecorp.com). It is governed by a BOD of which half consists of outsiders. For a privately held firm, this is a relatively uncommon, yet professional way to govern the business (Bloomberg.com 2018).

Director Compensation

In a large publicly held company, the compensation for directors can be quite large and ranges to hundreds of thousands of dollars, often with awards of stock in the company. In a smaller family business, some firms have begun paying directors the same daily rate as the company CEO. In the 6th Annual 2016 Private Company Board Compensation Survey by Lodestone Global and Forbes Magazine, the average retainer was $24,000 a year with $2,500 per meeting and $1,000 per telephone conference. In total, the median was $36,000 a year. Eighty-nine percent of private companies use cash and 34 percent use equity (stock). The survey reported that the average number of board seats was six with three outsiders. Fifty-seven percent of the boards had a woman member up from 55 percent the previous year. Fifty percent of the respondents of the survey were family-owned businesses. Nearly 50 percent of respondents rated the contribution of the board as indispensable or very effective at driving corporate strategy. The survey included 331 companies in 33 different industries and 39 countries (Tennenbaum 2016).

Duality of Roles: Chairman and CEO

In many firms, the chairman of the board also serves as the CEO. They are serving in dual roles. The BOD' responsibility is to provide oversight of the business. This responsibility includes oversight of upper management, including the CEO. The directors have hiring and firing authority over the CEO. It is not hard to see the conflict of interest in one person serving in both roles. However, in a family-owned firm or a family-controlled firm, it is especially common specifically among the first generation to have the founder serve in both these roles. The research has shown some conflicting results. However, the latest research shows that the CEO duality issue does not seem to be a problem with the first-generation founder-led organizations. It makes intuitive sense: The original entrepreneur and founder is the reason the firm is successful. The founder should be allowed to run the company as they see fit. The requirement to have an extra layer of decision making, oversight, and the resulting slowdown in communication would be a disadvantage to a small fast-growing organization. In a small founder-led firm, there is not much of a need for the oversight function of the chair of the BOD to be separated from the CEO. The data show that it becomes more of a problem in the later generations (Miller, Le Breton-Miller, and Lester 2011). Other research has shown eliminating the dual roles is not a "panacea" but it is a very complicated issue and one that needs consideration of many variables, such as how strong the leadership and TMT are, the generational stage, board compensation, executive compensation, and level of family control. Braun and Sharma (2007) found nonduality was negatively related to the level of family ownership. This is a counterintuitive finding and suggests rising ownership of nonfamily owners could create conflicts within the power structure itself and cause poor performance. They showed splitting the roles may reduce agency problem II, that of controlling owners negatively dominating over minority shareholders.

Warren Buffet has served on the boards of 19 public firms and believes the roles should be separated to avoid a conflict of interest. When the CEO is underperforming, the dual roles delay making a change in CEOs (Buffet 2014). As of 2018, Buffet's company Berkshire Hathaway Inc. had 14 members of their board. Of the 14, six are insiders, including Buffet, Jim Buffet (his son), and his partner Charlie Munger. Buffet, however, does serve in multiple roles at his company, as chairman of the board, president, and CEO. He has divided up key managerial roles among four business units. This is an example of the complexity of corporate governance. What works for one firm or may be thought of as a best practice, may not work for another firm. Buffet is widely believed to be one of the best, if not the best investor of all time. No one is suggesting that he not hold dual roles. The company has succeeded greatly because of him and there is no reason to change. The company grew to become one of the largest firms in the country because of his knowledge and skill. When Buffet retires, however, the positions will more than likely be occupied by several people (Berkshire Hathaway Inc. 2018).

In late 2018, Tesla CEO Elon Musk was sued by the SEC for comments made regarding a large Saudi investment in Tesla. The announcement made the stock rise, which hurt short sellers (those with options betting the firm would decline). The government accused him of manipulating the market. The settlement was a $20 million fine, the loss of his position as chairman of the board, and the forced addition of two independent members to the board (O'Kane 2018).

Board Committees

As part of their major responsibility, that of overseeing the TMT, there are several committees the directors participate in depending on their level of experience and familiarity. The very crucial audit committee is tasked with overseeing the financials and verifying they are accurate and represent the true financial standing of the business. Directors with financial expertise would be required for this committee. The compensation committee conducts research to benchmark effective and current pay scales for management and key employees. The nominating committee conducts research, recruits, and makes recommendations for future directors to join the board.

How the Board Interacts with the Family

The family council and the shareholder's council are the two main mechanisms of governance that interact with the board. The family council will elect a family member to represent the family's wishes and who will sit on the board as a full member/director. The council can request board updates. The shareholder council will be in communication with the board as well as with the TMT. It is at the shareholders annual meeting that the board members are elected or re-elected.

Insiders and Outsiders

In the past, controlling owners would often load their board with family members. In the case of the family-controlled firm, they would load it with friends and allies and a few key family members. This defeats the purpose of a strong and independent BOD that can provide oversight, offer advice, and make recommendations to management. The regulations now state there must be a balance of inside company directors and outside company directors. For publicly held, but family-controlled, firms, the New York Stock Exchange rules permit certain governance exemptions, such as a lower number of outsiders on family-controlled boards.

Multibillion-dollar worldwide media company and family-controlled News Corp is controlled by Rupert Murdoch and his family using two-tiered stock (Carr 2012). He has recently put his two sons on the board, Lachlan his heir apparent and his younger son James. James has a dual role of being a board member and serving as the CEO of 21st Century Fox. Murdoch himself held both the chairman and the CEO role recently (Carr 2012). With dual classes of stock, Murdoch controls a significant majority of the votes and can select board members for their loyalty. Out of the 11 board members, six can be considered insiders; Natalie Bancroft is a former opera singer and member of the Bancroft family who sold the *Wall Street Journal* to Murdoch. Jose Maria Aznar is the former president of Spain and a friend of Murdoch. Three of the board seats are filled by Murdoch and his sons, and five are *possibly* outsiders. As is commonly seen, the upper management roles are filled with family members

(Newscorp.com 2018). Each director makes over $200,000 per year in compensation (Carr 2012).

The family-controlled Estee Lauder Companies has 17 members on their BOD. Only five can be considered insiders, including four Lauder family members and the President and Chief Executive Officer Fabrizio Freda. It is interesting to note the wide variety of experience on the board: there is an attorney, several finance and banking experts, a tech expert, and Irvine Hockaday Jr., who was the president and CEO of Hallmark Cards, Inc., a family-owned company. This is important as he understands the complexities of a family business.

Estee Lauder Board of Directors (2018)

Charlene Barshefsky, Senior International Partner at WilmerHale

Rose Marie Bravo, CBE, Retail and Marketing Consultant

Wei Sun Christianson, Managing Director and Co-Chief Executive Officer of Asia Pacific and Chief Executive Officer of China at Morgan Stanley

Fabrizio Freda, President and Chief Executive Officer

Paul J. Fribourg, Chairman and Chief Executive Officer of Continental Grain Company

Mellody Hobson, President of Ariel Investments LLC

Irvine O. Hockaday Jr., former President and Chief Executive Officer of Hallmark Cards, Inc.

Jennifer Hyman, Co-Founder and Chief Executive Officer of Rent the Runway, Inc.

Leonard A. Lauder, Chairman Emeritus

Jane Lauder, Global Brand President, Clinique

Ronald S. Lauder, Chairman of Clinique Laboratories LLC

William P. Lauder, Executive Chairman

Richard D. Parsons, Senior Advisor of Providence Equity Partners LLC

Lynn Forester de Rothschild, Chair of E. L. Rothschild LLC

Barry S. Sternlicht, Chairman and Chief Executive Officer of Starwood Capital Group

Jennifer Tejada, Chief Executive Officer of PagerDuty, Inc.

Richard F. Zannino, Managing Director of CCMP Capital Advisors, LLC

Source: elcompanies.com.

Century-old, family-controlled Ford Motor company has 10 directors on its board including William Clay Ford Jr., the executive chairman, and Edsel B. Ford II. In addition, they have one other insider, the company President and CEO Jim Hackett (Ford.com 2018). Of the Ford board, 70 percent can be considered outsiders; however, the Ford family controls 40 percent of the votes with their super shares even though they only own approximately 2 percent of the stock (Muller 2010). This provides the family with a dominant amount of control.

Choosing Independent Directors

Family-business owners who had boards with two or more outside directors felt their boards had contributed to the effective management of their company. The following are the benefits of having outsiders on the board:

They provide an unbiased and objective view.

They bring with them an established network of contacts.

They bring a fresh and a broader perspective to important decision areas of the company.

(Adapted from Schwartz, and Barnes 1991, pp. 269–285)

See Appendix C for the International Finance Corporation Definition of an Independent Director.

Design and Creation of a BOD

Ideally, the family council will have created a written policy covering board member selection, which specifies the criteria for director selection as well as the process for recruitment, evaluation, and approval by the shareholders. By having the family council write this document, there should be some consensus agreement or *buy in* by a majority of the family members.

The best candidates for a board member are successful peers. CEOs and other high-level executives from other private or closely held companies would add value because they know the challenges of a closely held firm. It will also benefit family firms to have some directors from large Fortune 500 firms. The benefit of a board is the experience and knowledge each member brings. If a company was expecting an upcoming leadership succession to the next generation, it would be ideal to have someone on the board who has previously gone through the process. Similarly, if a business is considering expanding internationally; a board member with international experience would be highly desirable.

Board Evaluation

An area of improvement for family firms is with board evaluation. Few companies evaluate boards. Of those that do, research shows that the greater the evaluation of a board's performance, the better the company performs. Some firms use an evaluation questionnaire at the end of every director's tenure. Other firms interview board members and provide individual evaluations (Brenes et al. 2009). Family firms should do a better job conducting formal evaluations of their board's performance.

Statement of Corporate Governance

Most firms publish a document on their website discussing how the firm is governed and the responsibilities and procedures of the BOD (see Berkshire Hathaway's *Corporate Governance Guidelines* in Appendix A).

Summary

In summary, although the research on the increased professionalism and improved decision making with the usage of boards is clear, each family business is unique. There is no prescription for the best or ideal way to institute a BOD. All factors need to be taken into consideration, such as each family is different, industries are different, economies vary, family makeup varies, which generation is in control, size of the firm, and so on. The best way to institute a BOD would be to do what is best for that particular business and family.

Family-business managers and consultants should realize that increasing board size, activism, and the proportion of unaffiliated outsiders will not lead to improved performance under all conditions. It is important to reflect on the contingent situation created by various aspects of family involvement in the business (Corbetta and Salvato 2004, p. 132).

CHAPTER 6

Ownership Governance

There are two major tools for the governance of ownership: the shareholders council and the annual shareholders meeting (also called the annual shareholder meeting or the annual general meeting, AGM).

The Shareholders Council

The purpose of the shareholders council is to bring stockholders together to communicate, disseminate knowledge, and to make decisions by voting. The stockholders hear from upper management concerning the progress of the firm for the last quarter and their future plans for the business.

When a family firm is small, the family council will usually serve the purpose of the shareholders council. When the firm grows in sales, number of generations, and the number of shareholders, it becomes a prudent form of governance. The shareholder council becomes essential if the firm has any nonfamily shareholders or investors. Large companies may have both a shareholder council and a family council.

The family council differs from the shareholders council in that:

1. There may be nonfamily shareholders.
2. The family council is for *family* issues, and the shareholders council oversees business issues such as liquidity and profitability.

The most important tasks of the shareholders council are:

1. Oversight of the BOD, and
2. Delegation of the monitoring role of the TMT to the BOD

Other tasks of the shareholder council are to research possible candidates for future BOD members and forward their name to be voted on at the annual meeting by all shareholders. Succession of leadership will also be discussed at shareholder council meetings. The family council will take the primary lead on succession; however, if there are nonfamily shareholders, they will be interested in the best candidate for the job. Is that a family member? Or, is a nonfamily candidate the best choice? (Koberle-Schmid, Kenyon-Rouvinez, and Poza 2014).

The shareholder council would be elected for a certain term of years at the annual shareholder meeting. Most commonly the meetings would be held quarterly. The council would elect a chair who would be responsible for running the shareholder council meeting.

Example of When a Shareholder Council Is Needed

The Jones family business was started in 1967 by Ed Jones and his wife Margaret. They had four children. The business grew and the family now find themselves needing more financial capital. The family had an opportunity to take in a minority shareholder (another family) who were in the same social circle with the Jones family. The Jones family owns 75 percent of the firm, and the new shareholders own 25 percent. There is discussion among both families of going public by having an IPO of stock in the near future.

In the past, the business was governed by a family council when the second generation succeeded their parents. At the beginning of every year, they had an informal AGM to satisfy the requirements for the corporation. This structure worked well for their business and the siblings worked well together. Now, they have a new incoming family of seven members who will mix with the four second-generation Jones' family members, as well as nine members of the third-generation Jones' who have decided to enter the business. There will now be 20 stockholders in total.

By law, the Jones family will need to keep their family needs separate from those of the business to be fair to the minority shareholders. The family council will be retained and used to discuss issues important to the Jones family, and a shareholder's council will be created with members of both families. The shareholder council will meet quarterly, and each year the business will have a formal annual meeting where the stockholders will exercise their vote. This type of governance tool will serve two functions; the first is to help the company meet the requirements of treating all shareholders the same as well as professionalize their governance and corporate structure to prepare for an IPO.

Annual Shareholder Meeting

The annual shareholders meeting is required by law in most countries. As the company grows, the annual meeting will grow from the founder and immediate family to a meeting that can be quite large for multigenerational family firms. During the annual meeting, the entire group of shareholders elects the members to represent the family on the family council and shareholder council as well as approves members to serve on the BOD. It is the shareholders' right to elect the BOD. Then, the BOD sets the direction of the company. During the meeting, the shareholders will hear from the TMT about the progress the firm has made on its goals and objectives for the year. Dividends are proposed by the BOD and then approved by the shareholders. Capital improvements and debt obligations are also discussed.

Commonly, these meetings are held annually. This is easily understandable as some family firms can have hundreds of shareholders such as UK-based Clarks Footwear who had as many as 400 family stockholders and 2,000 employee stockholders (Cope 1997) and the 145 family stockholders of the 7th generation McIlhenny family of Tabasco sauce fame (Shevory 2007; Tabasco.com 2018). To meet more often, such as on a quarterly basis, would be impractical. This is the purpose of the shareholder council or the family council.

A fourth-generation family member and heir of the Stroh's Beer company attended an annual shareholders meeting and was shocked to hear from the family management that the firm would soon cease to exist as a going concern and dividend income would soon come to an end. She blames the failure on poor decision making by ingrained family leaders (Stroh 2016). This is an example of poor governance in action. If the company used more effective governance mechanisms to increase communication and transparency, this would not have been a surprise.

The institution of a family council and a shareholder's council would have disseminated proper communication much earlier and prevented family members from being blindsided at the annual meeting.

Example of an Agenda for an AGM

The agenda of the AGM will depend on the legal and governance structure of the organization, such as if the company is a private or public corporation, has a family council, or has a BOD. Annual shareholder meetings are typically scheduled just after the end of the fiscal year. This allows for the previous year's financial performance to be reviewed and discussed. By writing the BOD with their suggestions before the annual meeting, shareholders can shape the agenda.

The meeting agenda would be sent out with an announcement of the date of the annual meeting, usually 6 weeks in advance. Depending on the laws of the state in which the business is incorporated, some states require a certain number of shareholders to be present or vote by mail or proxy (give their vote to another member). Delaware, for example, requires a certain percentage will need to be present to have a valid meeting. Other states allow each business to set the number for a quorum in their corporate bylaws. The corporate bylaws also specify the timing and location of the annual meetings. In most cases, the meeting is held at the headquarters of the business itself or at a nearby hotel or conference center in the same city or one nearby.

The corporate secretary would take notes of the discussion and decisions (the minutes) during the meeting and have them prepared into document form to be disseminated and approved at the next meeting. Some states have a requirement that the minutes are disseminated shortly after (within weeks) the meeting.

A Basic Agenda Includes

1. Minutes from the last meeting
2. Appointment of new directors
3. Review of the financial statements
4. Any current or planned projects or current issues
5. The appointment of an auditor

6. Confirming the auditor's compensation
7. Nomination and confirming (by vote) of any directors to the board, members to the family council, and/or shareholders council

The annual meeting is also an opportunity for the board and the owners to review the strategic direction of the company. It is the time and place to review how and why decisions have been made and to discuss future issues/opportunities that may influence the direction and performance of the company.

For the Chair

Preparation is important so that the meeting runs smoothly and achieves its objectives. The chair needs to be well-briefed and prepared to facilitate the meeting effectively.

Sample Procedure for an AGM

- Chair: Call the meeting to order.
- Chair introduces self.
- Welcome all to the 2nd, 10th, 27th (etc.) Annual General Meeting of Smith Family Business Inc.
- Introduce other directors/trustees.
- Chairman says: "I confirm that under the Constitution/Corporate Bylaws of The Smith Family Business we have a quorum and I declare the meeting of shareholders/beneficiaries properly constituted."
- I advise the attendees that nonshareholders may be present (in-laws, spouses).
- As the notice of meeting (invitation to shareholders) has been circulated to all shareholders, I will take it as read.
- Proxies have been lodged by . . . shareholders holding . . . shares, representing . . . percent of the of the issued share capital of the company.
- "I advise that directors have confirmed that the minutes of the Annual General Meeting held on (date) are a true and correct record of that meeting. Copies of the minutes of the meeting are available at . . ."

1. Financial Statements and Auditors report "Ladies and Gentlemen, I move that we adopt the Financial Statements and Auditors report for the year ended (Date)."

- "I request a shareholder to second the motion. The motion is now open for discussion. Before inviting questions and discussion from shareholders, I shall briefly review the year."
- Give a brief report of key corporate activities.
- "I now invite questions from the floor."
- Put the motion to the meeting. "Call for those in favor to raise their right hand" (count raised hands) then those against. "Please raise your right hand" (count).
- (Declare the result of the vote).
  1. Auditor. I record the continuance in Office of the auditors, or I move the motion to reappoint the auditors, or, I move the motion to appoint new auditors (vote).
  2. Election of Director/s. "In accordance with the company's constitution Mr. John Smith II is retiring. Mr. John Smith III offers himself for election. His company experience and expertise will be invaluable to our company. I move that Mr. Smith be elected as a director of the company."
- "I request a shareholder to second the motion."
- "The motion is now open for discussion."
- Put the motion to the meeting, and vote.
  1. "Is there any other business?"
- There being no other business.
  1. I invite the Chief Executive to give a presentation now.
  2. Close meeting "That concludes the business of the meeting. I thank you for your attendance, I would like to remind all shareholders to join the BOD and the top management team for refreshments immediately after the meeting."

(Adapted from Template.net 2018)

Agenda for Small Family Business Shareholder Meeting

The following is a sample agenda for a privately held family-owned firm without a formal BOD or shareholder council.

8:00 a.m.	Breakfast
8:30 a.m.	Reconnect and discussion (informal)
9:00 a.m.	Review of company financials
10:00 a.m.	Discussion of important issues affecting the family
10:45 a.m.	Break
11:00 a.m.	Review/update shareholder agreement

Noon Lunch

1:00 p.m.	Discuss future successor development and family development
2:30 p.m.	Review estate plan
3:30 p.m.	Questions and new business
4:00 p.m.	Nomination and election of family council members
4:15 p.m.	Conclude meeting
5:30 p.m.	Social hour
6:30 p.m.	Family activity (fun)

PART III

Increasing the Professionalism of the Firm and the Role of Governance in the Future

CHAPTER 7

Increasing the Professionalism and Effectiveness of Family Firms

Improving Decision Making

For effective business performance, and for the continued success of the firm through multiple generations, decision making is a vital skill (Aronoff and Astrachan 1996; Alderson 2009). Decision making is a skill and it needs to be learned. For the next generation of family business members, some of the learning occurs in their professional education at college and by working for other companies before joining the family firm. Much of the learning takes place as they work at the company. Other learning takes place in the form of mentoring from one generation to another. History, values, and stories of the business are passed down by previous generations. If the previous generation does not effectively mentor and show how decisions are to be made and allow the next generation the freedom to make decisions to practice their decision-making effectiveness, decision making is likely to be poor, or delayed; at worst, it could be ineffective.

In the early days of the business, the controlling owner makes most or all the decisions. This can continue into future generations if there is a powerful controlling leader. This is very common in family business (Feltham, Feltham, and Barnett 2005). Research has shown groups of people are better decision makers than single individuals (Colquitt, LePine, and Wesson 2018). Instituting proper governance structures is a vital requirement to improving decision-making effectiveness. Having other people challenge the status quo or discuss new viewpoints when making decisions is a very effective way of increasing debate, discussion, and exploration of different and possibly *better* ideas. Having more interactions with a variety of people, especially experienced outsiders, helps increase the effectiveness of decisions. Boards of advisors, boards of directors, having family meetings, and instituting a family council are some of the governance tools that can help increase decision-making effectiveness.

As an example of improved decision making that could have an impact on profitability, Block (2010) showed that family-owned firms exhibited a reduced likelihood of employees being laid off in a downturn or recession. However, in a professionally managed family firm with proper governance structures installed, the likelihood of a layoff was the same as a nonfamily firm. This provides evidence that family-owned and family-managed firms often practice altruism when they are able. This provides evidence for the socioemotional approach as family owners care more about their reputation in the community. By having professional management and governance, the firm acts in a more professional manner.

Improving Communication and Preventing Conflict

Communication is an area of improvement for many families, especially those families in business with each other. Many families do not have a healthy way of communicating, and this can lead to conflict. Proper governance tools allow for increased dissemination of information and ideas and foster increased discussion. When members can voice their view concerning an issue, and feel they have been heard and treated fairly, even if the discussion and eventual decision does not align with their views, there is an increased amount of acceptance or "buy in" for the decision. It is best for families in business together to have an agreement that decisions are supported by all and that discord is not propagated outside of the discussion. By having buy in with decisions, the family can speak with a unified voice and prevent dissent. This helps to prevent destructive conflict. Conflict can occur when people have serious concerns about an issue and occurs regularly when those concerns are not addressed. Good governance structures enable positive channels of communication, which can head off conflict.

Family Business Professionals and Consultants

There are many professionals who often specialize in helping families in business, such as family business consultants, family therapists and counselors, accountants, insurance professionals, lawyers, tax attorneys, and estate planners.

Many family firms do not utilize professional family business consultants. Some may not know the role exists. These professionals are often scholars or researchers, and some have been certified as a family business practitioner by the Family Firm Institute (FFI). Others came from the finance or estate planning fields and specialize in family-owned businesses.

When a family business has a crisis of succession, they often reach out to a family business professional for help. As discussed earlier, it is very late to be asking for help. Another time family firms utilize consultants is when they have intractable interpersonal conflict between family members and it has become destructive. Often, the family business consultants have an entire team of family business professionals, so they can handle all aspects of a client's needs. The consultants all have a psychologist or family therapist/counselor either on staff or one they can recommend. Many would be surprised at the myriad of family issues a counselor deals with at family firms. Once a family utilizes a family business professional, they form a relationship built on trust and the consultant becomes a valued advisor at many firms. It is priceless for the business to have the benefit of experienced and knowledgeable professionals who have gone through similar situations before.

Accountants are extremely important to family-owned businesses, especially in the founder's tenure. They were found to be the most trusted advisor for small firms. Having a good working relationship with an accountant who can communicate well is a requirement, especially for the founding entrepreneur who may not be comfortable with financial statements and how to read and analyze them. The local banker is important in this regard as well when firms are small.

Insurance agents and estate planners are important to have a proper plan in place and an insurance benefit for the inevitable death of a key family member or family CEO, which could trigger tax and estate issues. The estate planner can create a long-term estate plan to decrease taxes and ensure the wealth passes on to family members. Buy–sell agreements are financed by life insurance and insure key family members. The family buys life insurance policies on each other, and when there is a death, the beneficiaries can buy their company shares from the departed family member and possibly pay for any taxes using the life insurance proceeds. As an example, the O'Malley family, the former owners of the Los Angeles Dodgers, were forced to sell their beloved team after the death of their longtime controlling owner and patriarch of the family and had to pay a significant tax burden. Good estate planning is vital to intergenerational success of the family firm. Mostly, all family business consultants will have recommendations for tax, life insurance, and estate specialists who are knowledgeable of the unique nature and issues of a family business and can help safeguard its success.

The choice of governance structures and mechanisms depends on a variety of factors. Each family business is unique, and each family is different. Installing certain governance mechanisms will depend on the family, their culture, their goals, the size of the family and the business, what generation of leadership they are presently, company age, complexity, and so on. Governance is specific to each company. One size does not fit all when it comes to governance. A family must do what is right for their specific situation.

Stakeholder Management

To know and understand the needs, interests, and expectations of various stakeholders of the family business, company management needs to have relationships with the important stakeholders. Some businesses have created a position to engage stakeholders: the corporate stakeholder relationship director. Their purpose is to communicate with stakeholders and then inform management of their interests (Institute of Directors in Southern Africa 2016).

Family Offices

One of the faster growing trends among family businesses has been the use of family offices. As the business matures, it becomes more complex, with several generations of ownership and multiple families involved. At the same time, the business continues to grow, and family members' wealth increases to significant amounts. This creates the need to have a professional *family office* to take care of the needs of the families Murray, Gersick, and Lansberg (2001/2002). Usually the office is recommended by the corporate attorney, who becomes concerned about the amount of comingling of the family's needs with those of the business. Inception of a family office also becomes necessary when several groups of owners with varying amounts of shares, sometimes nonvoting, are involved. The need also occurs when the family diversifies and becomes a group of family trusts, limited partnerships, corporations, or holding companies and has members with a variety of different investments. As the family business grows, its need for professional and personal services also grows. Family offices normally house the family charitable foundation and are where the family often combines its wealth or investment funds for outside investments. Most often, these offices are operated by professional management.

Events such as an IPO, an acquisition, or a divesture may increase demands for professional services or for cash. When a family business is divested or sold, family members often use the family office as a way to keep the family together, maintain their leverage and power by investing as a group, access financial and legal services at no or low cost, and keep the family legacy alive. Family offices are dynamic and change as the family grows and transitions. Private wealth management and investment firms are now targeting the family office as a very large key customer.

A more advanced type of family office is a multifamily office (MFO). This is where several separate families unite under a single-family office. The Pitcairn family of the PPG fortune (Pittsburgh Plate Glass Company) sold their PPG holdings, and most of the 200-plus family members have stayed in business together through their Pitcairn Trust Company, an MFO that manages the Pitcairn family money, as well as those of other wealthy families and individuals. Using professional wealth management professionals, the firm has been able to generate higher than average returns on capital. The trust often invests in large publicly owned family businesses because of their long-term strategies and above-average financial results.

CHAPTER 8

The Future of Governance

The future of corporate governance is an increasing level of transparency. Since the dot-com bust of the 1980s and 1990s, the financial scandals of WorldCom, Tyco, and Enron and the advent of the Sarbox financial accountability legislation, there has been an increased emphasis on more transparency. Transparency regarding finances and accounting has been the focus, but also, an increased emphasis on being as transparent as can be on many other issues affecting the organization. For example, because of human rights issues abroad, many companies have reported steps they have taken to make sure their suppliers are treating employees safely without abuse. The advent of numerous social media platforms has created a need for significant transparency. Businesses cannot conceal their actions in secret (Institute of Directors in Southern Africa 2016).

Many companies now report on their sustainability regarding their purchasing. This is done to show consumers and other stakeholders they are not harming the environment or taking advantage of suppliers in developing countries. A 156-year-old family firm Bacardi Limited now publishes their environmental sustainability report. The report was based on stakeholder input, and shows corporate progress on areas such as reduction in greenhouse gas emissions, water usage, waste, packaging, and their commitment to buying from sustainable supplier partners (Bacardi Limited 2018).

The State of California created legislation in 2012 requiring companies doing businesses in California to disclose the social responsibility of their suppliers (JD Supra 2011; see Chick-fil-A statement of transparency in Appendix B).

Concern for Stakeholders

The reason for the rise in transparency is an increased concern for stakeholders. This concern is twofold; regulating bodies are increasing demands that all stakeholders be treated fairly, as well as increased knowledge and activism on the part of many consumers. For example, consumers want complete information regarding where their fish was caught. Was it caught using sustainable fishing practices? Consumers are asking where their products were made or assembled and what the human rights records are of members in a company's supply chain.

SC Johnson, now in its fifth generation of family management, publishes a list of the ingredients used in its products. It started in 2009 and now includes information in 34 languages, in 52 countries, covering 5,300 products (SC Johnson.com n.d.-b). Consumers demanded information regarding their exposure to chemicals and the company responded with transparency.

Corporate Social Responsibility

The above-mentioned issues can be combined into a demand for increased corporate responsibility. Many companies now have an office of corporate social responsibility (CSR) and are tasked with making sure the company acts in a responsible manner in all endeavors. Many publish a statement on their website concerning their CSR standards and what steps they are taking to be a responsible corporate citizen. This is being driven in large part by an increasingly vocal and active consumer base (Niehm, Swinney, and Miller 2008).

Asian Family Businesses

Most of the economic growth for the rest of the century will be from counties like China and India among several others. In those countries, there is a proliferation of family-owned firms (Susanto and Susanto 2013). Often, successful families have several businesses in multiple industries. These families often dominate their economies, have a long-term orientation, outcompete their rivals, and will likely be responsible for the majority of the world's economic growth for several decades (Björnberg, Elstrodt, and Pandit 2015; McKinsey Global Institute 2014, 2015; Tsao et al. 2018; Wang 2010).

Women in Family Business

In the last few decades, there has been a large increase in the number of women being involved in their own family business. In a 2007 survey by MassMutual Financial Group, 24 percent of surveyed family firms in 2007 had a woman CEO, up from only 10 percent in 2002. Thirty-four percent of CEOs surveyed said the company's next CEO might be a woman. According to the study, these are substantial businesses, having $26.9 million in average annual revenues, with some reporting $1 billion in sales. Moreover, the report stated that women-owned businesses were more likely to focus on succession planning, to have a 40-percent lower rate of family-member attrition, to be more fiscally conservative, and to carry less debt than male-owned businesses. In 1994, according to another survey, 2 percent of CEOs in family businesses were women. In 2005, 9.5 percent of family business heads were women (MassMutual 2007).

In a 2015 study by the consulting firm Ernst & Young consisting of 525 of the World's largest and oldest family-owned firms, 70 percent of surveyed respondents stated they were considering a woman for their next CEO, and 30 percent said they were strongly considering a woman for the position. Fifty-five percent reported at least one woman on the board, and 16 percent of board members were women. In a positive development, 22 percent of firms stated 22 percent of their top management is comprised of women, compared with only 12.9 percent average of all firms in general (EY 2015).

Working with Nonfamily Management

An area of improvement for family firms is better utilization of nonfamily management. This is a requirement if the business is to grow to scale and become as successful as it could be. The governance mechanisms of the company should consider how they treat nonfamily members, including compensation, promotions, communication, and levels of trust. Decision-making authority should be clearly spelled out. Often family firms ignore the decision-making hierarchy, which frustrates nonfamily management as well as outsiders (Kets de Vries 1993). Personnel decisions are often made from the point of view of the family values and personality issues, instead of standard performance criteria (Welsch 1996). To keep nonfamily employees and managers motivated and committed to the organization, they need to be treated well. Employees want to know how they will be evaluated, compensated, and promoted. They often wonder if there is a career path for them at a family firm. Proper governance procedures can help increase the professionalism of the family firm and make communication and decision making clearer for all.

Future Research

Much of the governance literature and family business governance research has been on U.S.-based firms. Because the growth of the global economy is tilting toward Asia, more research should be conducted on governance in the Chinese and Indian family businesses. Asian countries have a more collective culture rather than the individualistic cultures seen in the West. How does that affect governance?

Considering the rise of women in family business, more should be learned regarding differences they may have in choosing governance tools. Are they more open to governance mechanisms? Regarding the stakeholder and SEW approaches, and the vital relational aspects of family members, more research should be undertaken to understand at a deeper level on the varying motivations and ideals of individual family members. Are they humanistic? Materialistic? Individualistic? Religious? (Dyck and Schroeder 2005).

Nonfamily employees and managers are key to the successful operation of family firms. More research needs to be done regarding how the company can best encourage them and take advantage of their skills and experience. A family constitution, family council, and shareholder meetings may decide how family members are promoted and to whom they should report. Nonfamily management needs to see a career path at the firm. If they suspect rampant nepotism, they will leave.

The entire domain of family business suffers from a lack of an agreed-upon definition of what constitutes a family business. There is certainly a vast difference between a small completely owned family business versus a very large public family-controlled business listed on the S&P 500. At a minimum, the researcher conducting a study should clarify their specific definition of family business. The specific generation in control should be listed and discussed because this has been shown to influence governance structures and performance.

The evidence has been inconclusive regarding the performance of family-owned and family-controlled businesses and how they compare with their nonfamily counterparts. The difference may lie in the conflicting definitions of what is a family firm. More research needs to be performed in this vitally important area. If the superior financial performance of family firms is found to be true, it could change many people's views of family businesses. The most important result may be a change in governmental policies to support and encourage family firms. Family businesses, based on the size of their contribution to the economies around the world should be supported and encouraged.

For Further Thought and Discussion

- Identify what stage your company occupies: Is the first-generation founder still in control? Have the second or third generation taken control? Assess the company size, age, and number of employees. What governance tools are used now? This is vital to know what governance mechanisms to utilize.
- Are you a member of a family that owns a company? What are some of the main challenges facing your company and your family?
- Are you a nonfamily senior executive in a family-owned company? List some of the larger challenges facing the firm.
- Based on the discussions in this book, identify specific steps toward resolving these challenges, using corporate governance practices.

Conclusion

Governance is the key to increased professionalism and proper management of the family firm. Financial performance under the founder of a family firm is usually quite good. Miller and Le Bretton-Miller (2005, 2006) show numerous instances of family firms financially outperforming nonfamily firms. Data show the second and third generation family CEOs have not enjoyed a similar amount of financial outperformance as their family predecessors (Miller, Le Breton-Miller, and Lester 2011). This shows the increased need for proper governance in the second, third, and future generations. If the second and third generations do not institute effective governance structures and professional management and instead continue to try and run the firm as the founder did, the result is usually slowed growth. The best managed family firms have increased professionalism with the utilization of proper governance tools.

As discussed, the choice of which governance tools to use depends on several factors, including what generation is in control, the number of involved family members, the size of the firm, its complexity, and whether the company is family owned or family controlled. There is no one single answer as to what mechanism or type of governance is best. The answer is *it depends*. It depends on the ownership structure and numerous company-specific factors. What works at one stage of the ownership cycle usually does not work well at other stages. Families in control should take a cautious look at the governance solutions recommended for their specific stage and decide what is best for their company and their family (IFC 2008).

For example, a small one-generation family-owned firm would be fine with the founder CEO making almost all the decisions and running the company as they see fit. This is the type of simple and informal governance structure needed for this type of firm to excel. The founder is the person who has the passion for the business, having started it and led it successfully. This type of firm would benefit from a lack of formal governance mechanisms until it advanced to a larger size, involved more family members, or approached the start of a succession of leadership. Conversely, a large public company controlled by a family would benefit by having many governance mechanisms, including a strong and independent BOD, a separate CEO role from the chairman's role, a family council, and a shareholders council. Experienced non-family CEOs can add to the professionalism of a large and growing family controlled firm (Blumentritt, Keyt, and Astrachan 2007).

Case Studies

Case Study One
The Sibling Power Struggle

Otto Cresmer founded the Cresmer Manufacturing Company (CMC) in 1955 upon his immigration to the United States following World War II. He was an engineer in his home country of Switzerland. He and his wife, Katarina, started CMC. CMC designed radio tubes and eventually television tubes for the expanding postwar markets.

Over the years the company had to endure the loss of market share as new technologies were developed such as the transistor and the silicon chip, which rendered the company products obsolete. However, Otto's core competency was in product design, and he continued to create new products that met the needs of newly developing and growing markets. The company is now the world's largest provider of electrical components for the marine, auto navigation, and GPS industries. Sales have totaled $119 million for fiscal 2017, an increase of 9 percent over 2016.

Otto and his wife had three children, all of whom entered the family business. John, the oldest at 47, was an accountant and serves as vice president (VP) of finance. He joined the company 11 years ago. Sandra, who has an MBA from Columbia, is VP of sales and marketing and previously worked at large advertising firms and did a stint at Proctor and Gamble in product management before joining the family business 7 years ago. Jackie is a manufacturing engineer like her father; she joined the company 3 years ago after working for several small Silicon Valley startups. She is the most well-off family member, having received several hundred thousand stock options in her former firm that went public. She is the VP of manufacturing. Ken, the youngest at 34, is most like his father, who can be hotheaded and stubborn. Ken is a former musician who now wants to join the company.

Part One

"I don't know what we are going to do regarding the kids," Otto said to his wife. "I thought it would be great to have all the children together, but with Ken joining the company, we now have out-and-out sibling warfare. I told Ken he could join the company, and now all the others are mad at me. Jackie is not speaking with me, and John and Sandra are screaming at each other."

"Well, Otto, you know how close Sandra is with Ken, she has a soft spot for him, just as you do," said his wife.

"I know," Otto said, "it's just that he has not had it as easy as the others." Otto was referring to Ken's previous drug usage and arrests. "When he was in the band it was pretty prevalent, and he got caught up in the whole 'rock star' thing, but he has been clean now for 3 years. I think it would be wonderful for him to join the company. The problem is he announced it to the others before I could, and said he was going to be a VP."

"A VP of what?" Katarina exclaimed.

"I did not tell him he was going to be a VP," said Otto.

"Good!" said Katarina, "no wonder the children are upset; they all have good college degrees and work experience under their belts, and Ken has none of that."

"Oh, said Otto, he's just getting a late start."

"There you go again!" said Katarina. "You always favored Ken."

With that comment, the discussion broke up and Otto stalked out of the room.

Part Two

"Hi Mom," said John, "can we talk?"

"Of course, said Katarina.

"It's this thing with Ken," said John. "I just do not understand it. We have all worked hard to be in the positions we have, and for Dad to bring in Ken at a VP level with no experience is . . . ."

"I know," said Katarina, "but to be fair, it's the family business, and we feel it's for all the children. And, just to let you know, your father did not tell Ken he was going to be a VP."

"Well what do you call being put in charge of design?" asked John.

"What?" Katarina replied.

"Yeah, evidently he is our new design chief! Jackie is ticked! She is well off, she does not need this drama. She is actually thinking of leaving."

"Oh my!" said Katarina, "I'll talk with your father about this, John."

"Thanks, Mom," John said.

A few minutes later, the phone rings. "Hi Mom," said Sandra.

"Oh, hi, honey," Katarina replied.

"Mom, this thing with Ken has gotten out of hand. I am a big fan of his joining the company, but not at that high of a level; it is just not right. He needs to earn it. I still remember when the police . . ."

"All right," said Katarina, "we all remember that. It was a long time ago."

"Not long enough, Mom. Our reputation is at stake. If this gets out among our key customers, I cannot overcome the ding on our reputation. Our competitors will make a huge deal out of this."

"OK, honey, I will talk with your Dad about this."

"Thanks, Mom; by the way, have you spoken with Jackie yet? No? Well, she stormed out last night, shouting life is too short; I think her and Brian are flying to France this morning to rest and cool off."

"France? I'll talk with your father," Katarina said.

Katarina calls Jackie on the phone. "Jackie? Hi."

"Hi, Mom," Jacki said. "I don't have a lot of time, we are packing for a trip.

"I heard" Katarina said.

"Oh?"

"Yes, your sister called me and told me you were upset.

"Upset? I am not upset! I am livid!" Jackie screamed into the phone.

"Well honey, we will get this figured out," said Katarina.

"No, Mom, there is nothing to figure out. Dad gave Ken a key position in my department, and I will not oversee him. I have all the responsibility but no authority! And I am not going to be responsible for that drug-addicted, no good . . ."

"Now, Jackie," Katarina interrupted, "it has been a few years, he is clean and served his time.

"Served his time? Dad bought him a great lawyer who had him serve his time at a beach resort rehab hospital. I am not dealing with him. I cannot believe Dad would give away a vital position in my department without talking to me! I have to go now, Mom."

"OK, honey," Katarina said, "just know, I will speak with your father about this."

Part Three

Ken stopped by Otto's office later that day. "Dad, why is everyone mad at me? John and Sandra aren't speaking to me, and Jackie is nowhere to be found."

"Well, Ken, I wanted to give you a chance here, you deserve it. Our business is open to all family members. I thought design would be the best place for you, with your creative mind, but I did not have a chance to discuss it with the others first. That was my plan. You jumped the gun and told them instead. I should have been the one to tell them. And you told them you were going to be a VP!"

"Well, we had discussed that," said Ken.

"Yes," Otto said, "but that was going to be after a few years, and after everything settled in."

"Well, everyone else is a VP," said Ken.

Questions

1. What are the issues? From the sibling's point of view? From Otto's?

2. What do you see as the key problems?

3. If you were a family business consultant, what advice would you give? To Otto? To the family?

Case Study Two

The Missing in Action Brother

The BNC Corporation was established in 1969 by Joseph Colby. It had enjoyed tremendous success both domestically and internationally and was doing $200 million a year in annual sales. It was firmly in the hands of the second generation with Joseph's two children, Robert, 45, and Jolene, 43. Robert is the president and CEO, and Jolene is the vice president for sales and marketing. The company is privately held, with Robert and Jolene sharing 75 percent of the shares, and Joseph and his wife with 25 percent.

Robert and his wife had been having marriage problems on and off for many years. In 2013, the pair decided to separate. Robert took this hard, became depressed, and started to abuse alcohol. His performance at the company started to decline. He started missing a day or two here and there, then multiple days in a row. In June of 2014, he did not come to work and would not answer his phone.

Jolene had no choice but to take over some of Robert's responsibilities. At first, she thought it would be temporary and Robert would be coming back. She continued to pay his salary until the checks came back as undeliverable. He was nowhere to be found. Three years later, owing to Jolene's hard work, the company was more successful than ever. Sales were now approaching $600 million annually. Jolene saved Robert's ownership dividends in an account to be given to him at some point in the future.

In June of 2017, Robert arrived at the company, seemingly as if nothing had changed, and wanted to resume his previous job. He wondered why his sister was driving the expensive luxury car he saw in her parking spot. He also demanded a job for his young girlfriend.

Questions

1. What are the associated risks and problems with Robert coming back?

2. If you were Jolene, how would you feel?

3. What are the options in this situation?

4. If you were a family business owner or consultant, what would you advise?

5. What should Jolene do?

Case Study Three
The Out-of-the-Loop Family Shareholder

Mary Smith is 61 years old and is an owner and former employee (for 20 years) of Smith Mechanical Inc. in Minneapolis, Minnesota, the firm her father, Sam Smith, started. The firm does approximately $15 million in sales annually. Mary's husband, Don, developed medical issues, and they felt the need to move to a drier climate for his health. It has been 3 years since Mary and her husband left the company employment. She used to enjoy daily chats with her father and brothers, but now only gets short e-mails providing brief information regarding the company.

Her father, a certified engineer, is semiretired. He has slowly been turning the management and leadership of the firm over to his two sons. Mary's older brother, Robert, has an MBA and is responsible for sales and marketing. Her younger brother, Peter, graduated 7 years ago with a mechanical engineering degree and is now in charge of production. The company has, over many years, successfully carved out a niche in aircraft parts and has recently expanded internationally. To reduce their dependence on a single industry, the brothers and their father together decided to enter other industrial markets. The investment has been costly, and profits are down.

Over the years, the dividends have been cut twice, and now there is talk of suspending the shareholders' dividends altogether. She has become increasingly angrier at her family and the decisions they are making as it has put her retirement income at risk, especially since she no longer has employment income from the company.

She has had several phone conversations with her father and her two brothers, and has increasingly grown more confrontational and hostile. The last one ended with her hanging up the phone on her brother.

She has considered hiring a lawyer to protect her interest in what she now considers to be a company that is increasingly mismanaged by her two brothers.

Questions

1. What is the real problem Mary is experiencing?
2. Could it have been prevented? How can it be managed?
3. Should Mary and Don be treated as one?
4. What governance needs does the family and business have?

Case Study Four

The Substance Abusing Family Employee

The Kenney Manufacturing Company is an Ohio-based family business situated in a farming region of Ohio. It is one of the largest private employers in the state with over 3,500 employees. It is the biggest employer in the local region and a manufacturer of farm equipment. It has been in business for over 75 years. The Kenney Manufacturing Company is 100 percent owned by three sibling partners from the second generation. The children of the owners all work in the business as well.

Issue: One of the third-generation family members who has a rumored substance abuse problem crashes the company truck into a fire truck responding to a fire in the local downtown area near their corporate headquarters. Several people are injured. Because the Kenney family has significant regional and statewide importance, the story is covered by the news media. The company has significant liability for the accident, as well as public relations damage to the family name as it is associated with this event.

Two of the sibling partners are livid and want to terminate the family employee who was in the accident. The family has a constitution that states the remedy for the first offence of the substance abuse policy is that the employee must undergo counseling. The two partners do not feel this is enough. The family members knew in advance about the existence of the substance abuse problem, and so did the public. They feel the business is at great risk owing to this event and that quick action is called for. They have called an emergency meeting of the BOD to discuss the situation.

The situation becomes more complex day by day. Reporters and TV trucks are parked outside the company headquarters daily and are holding a vigil at the local hospital for the injured. The daily newspaper carried a story headlined "Kenney Heir at Fault in Serious Crash" after a drug test came back positive and was leaked to the press. The town is angry after the family member posted a million-dollar bail owing to the family's significant wealth. Local farmers are canceling their orders. The company's salespeople cannot get their customers on the phone. The word "toxic" has been suggested by some of the customers if they were to buy from the company.

Questions

1. What should be done regarding the employee at fault?
2. Could this have been prevented?
3. If you were on the BOD, what would you do to mitigate this situation?
4. Is the constitution effective as it is presently written?
5. Assess the strength of their governance procedures.

Case Study Five
Early Stage Pressure

Marc Watson started his software development company 5 years ago while working for a large high-tech company. It is now doing 5.7 million in annual sales and is 100 percent privately held by Marc and his wife. The company is run from a small facility in Southern California. His two children, Arlena, 25, and Mitchell, 23, have worked at the company since they graduated from college. Arlena studied computer science, and Mitchell has a business degree and is presently pursuing an MBA. The two have been pushing for more of a say in the business as their father makes all the decisions without much input from them. They want their father to have regular family meetings, a family constitution, and form a family council. In addition, they would like to have a board of advisors to gather ideas and advice from a broader perspective. Mark is 49 years old, feels as full of energy as the day he started the firm, and sees no scenario where he would reduce his control and decision-making authority (especially to his relatively inexperienced children). Presently, they have no outside managers. Sales are conducted directly online by a sales force of commissioned agents, and there are only 12 employees.

Questions

1. Is Marc wrong?
2. What stage is this company presently?
3. Do you see a need for governance for the family at this time? For the business?

Case Study Six

Large Family Rumors

Nancy Lloyd was on the phone with her cousin Mary and remarked that the family had gotten so big and, what with all the marriages and grandchildren in the past few years, she did not know who was who anymore.

Mary agreed: "Remember when we used to have quick family meetings when we were small when our dads ran the company? Now we get an e-mail or a newsletter. One of Bob's kids is now in management; I do not even know who he is!"

"Oh," said Nancy, "that's Jake. He has an MBA from one of those prestigious universities back east. He is sharp."

"How do you know that?" Mary asked.

"Oh, Bob and I talked last Christmas," Nancy replied.

"Well, I heard he got fired from his last job for a DUI." Said Mary. "And another thing," Mary said. "I heard we aren't going to get any dividends this year due to the high costs of that new machinery they bought."

"Oh! I hadn't heard that," said Nancy. "That's going to hurt; we just put the girls in private school; I hope that's not true."

Questions

1. What is the problem here?
2. What aspect of governance could be improved here—the business, the family, or the owners?
3. What can be done to alleviate their concerns?
4. What can be done to prevent misinformation in the future?

Case Study Seven
The Overbearing Patriarch

Michael Snyder was the founder and main owner of Snyder Systems, a fast-growing software company specializing in data management and security. He started the firm and grew it to over $25 million in sales. Now that his children were becoming involved, they wanted more communication, more transparency, and more of a say in decisions. Michael had recently started gifting his children stock as an estate planning tool. He owned 75 percent of the company, and his four children owned the remainder.

The family business consultant recommended a family council be instituted to increase the level of shared decision-making and to increase communication. That was 2 years ago. Michael is not excited about reducing his power in decision-making. After all, he thought, "I am the one that built this company. What do they know? I am not going to give them a say in my decisions."

Questions

1. What problems are occurring?
2. Do you see more problems occurring in the future?
3. How can both Michael and the children be satisfied?
4. Make recommendations using governance tools to improve the situation.

Case Study Eight
Being Heard

The Target Acquisition Group is a large family-owned real estate investment firm started in 1975 by John and Samantha Sanchez. It had a successful generational succession of leadership from the first to the second generation of the family. John is chairman of the board, and his three children are all officers and in management at the firm. There are nine grandchildren, ranging in age from 27 to 39. The firm had been run by John and his wife until the recent succession only 3 years ago. The second generation feels as if they paid their dues while working hard collecting rents and developing properties and are now enjoying being in control and the fruits of their labor. The business has been very successful as the family has considerable real estate holdings in some of the nicer areas along the California coast.

The third generation is chafing under the patriarchal and authoritarian style of management. They want a larger say in the business and more participative decision-making. They are also not happy about some family members being treated differently than others. For example, some family members are driving Fords as company cars, and others Lexus and BMWs.

Questions

1. What is the problem or situation?
2. What can be done here?
3. Are government mechanisms the answer?
4. Does the company need to bring in outside resources?
5. What can be done to enable the second generation to "share power"? Should they? Or is the third generation feeling entitled?

Case Study Nine
The Inattentive Board

Smith Laboratories is a 48-year-old manufacturer and wholesaler of chemical compounds used in the beauty industry. When Steve Smith first formed the company, it was difficult and he had many sleepless nights. It was a financial struggle for many years. Over the long term, the company has prospered and grown. Now in its second generation of family leadership, the company is experiencing some problems with its BOD. The directors are paid well, yet seem unprepared and lack initiative. When succession was discussed at the last board meeting, there was some murmuring that the successor should not be a family member. The family representatives on the board were dismayed as they fully desire the next CEO to be a family member. They engaged in a successor development program a decade ago. The potential successor went to college, one is an engineer, one has an MBA, and the other is an accountant.

The board was formed by Steve Smith 20 years earlier, right after the succession to the second generation. Most of the same board members are still serving on the board. Stan is the chairman of the board, his son is CEO and has run the company successfully, expanding its product lines through organic growth as well as positive acquisitions. The son grew the company from $12 million in sales when he succeeded his father to over $97 million presently. It is the desire of Steve, his son, and the entire family that the company be run by a family member.

The family has a constitution and utilizes a family council to make decisions that concern the family and present their decisions to the board. All the members of the board are friends or business associates of Steve Smith. Their ages range from 60 to 81. They include the company accountant and the owner of the local bank that Smith Labs has used for over 30 years.

Questions

1. Assess how well the company is utilizing the various governance tools at its disposal?
2. What do you think about the composition of the board?
3. Concerning the governance mechanisms used, is Smith Labs currently structured well, considering its size, generation, and age?
4. What would you change and why?

Case Study Ten

Gaining Wisdom

Future Technologies Inc. is a family-owned technology company with proprietary software for the aerospace and transportation industries. When Stan Moore and his wife, Susan, ran the company by themselves they had efficient and quick decision-making. If they needed advice, they spoke with their accountant or their banker. All three of Stan and Susan's children entered the business after graduating from college in engineering, marketing, and finance, and after working elsewhere for a few years. Stan felt it was important that they find success on their own before entering the family business.

On the advice of a family business consultant, they wrote a family constitution and formed a family council. They instituted an informal board of advisors of respected business people and professionals. The second generation worked for 15 years before Stan and Susan decided to slow down and begin the succession process. The family council created a succession identification plan. Eventually, the two older siblings were seen as CEO material and were interested in the position. The choice of CEO will be the biggest test of the governance mechanisms put in place by the family. The family hired a family business consultant, who assessed the capabilities of each of the candidates and prepared a report. The report, presented at a family council meeting, stated that the two candidates were comparable in strengths and weaknesses and suggested some assignments outside of their regular areas of responsibilities to gain important experience. The son went to Europe to start an international division, and the daughter moved from finance to operations.

Stan and Susan became increasingly uncomfortable with making a choice between the two siblings for the next CEO. They were concerned the one not chosen would be upset and feel less loved than the other. They felt it was reasonable, on the basis of their sales growth and size of firm (they were approaching $1 billion in sales), to create a BOD. On the advice of their consultant, board members were recruited on the basis of their strengths matching the needs of the firm. The board consisted of:

- An outside director from a large family-controlled firm that had recently gone public.

- An outside director from a large family-owned firm that had successfully undergone a leadership succession.
- An outside director from a large Fortune 500 firm who was vice president (VP) of marketing.
- An outside director from a large family firm who recently led an expansion internationally.
- A VP of finance from a large Fortune 500 firm.
- Stan served as the board chairman.
- The head of the family council was a nonvoting member of the BOD.

It was seen by the family as another step in the professionalism of the business. In a family council meeting, both potential CEO candidates agreed to be bound by the recommendation of the board. Recently, Stan and Susan have begun to have second thoughts about hurt feelings and have considered a co-CEO position to be shared by both their children.

Questions

1. Do you think the creation of the board will be successful in helping choose the next leader?
2. What are the possibilities of hurt feelings among family members?
3. Does the board have the right composition to help the company for the future?
4. What do you think about the co-CEO idea?
5. What should Stan and Susan do?

Case Study Eleven

The Absentee Owner and the In-Law

The Carlucci vineyards is a thriving business now in its second generation. Bob Carlucci is CEO and president; his sister, Anna, is VP. Their parents founded the firm in the 1970s. The parents are co-chairs of the board. On weekends, the vineyard is known for having the most popular wine tasting room in the area. The tasting room is crowded, with standing room only, and often full, with an overflowing crowd outside. The firm has grown well under Bob's leadership, with sales totaling $12 million a year, up from $2.7 million when Bob took over. Bob lives on the property, and that is one reason why the tasting room is so popular. He works 12-hour days. He loves his job and will often drop by the tasting room to mingle with the guests. Since he lives on the property, he can "sense" when business is off by the sheer volume of voices coming from the tasting room.

The stock is evenly split three ways between Bob, his sister, and their parents, each having 33 1/3 percent. Bob earns a salary for his hands-on role in running the operation. His sister Anna, who lives in the northern part of the state and visits irregularly, receives dividends. Anna's husband has been very vocal about reports, data, and spreadsheets being sent to them weekly and monthly, asserting that they needed to have a full picture of what was going on at the company, and has pushed for changes in the way the company was run. The couple was also upset with Bob for "basically running everything without their input." Conversely, Bob was livid at their request for reports. "If they want to know something, maybe they should get off their tails and come down here and see for themselves," Bob stated.

A family business consultant was brought in. The first recommendation was to institute a family council with regular meetings. The family business consultant was utilized as the facilitator. Ann and her husband readily agreed since they would now have a say in decisions.

Later, when discussing the effectiveness of the family council, Bob stated he still did what he wanted to do but that it just took longer. He now had to wait for a meeting of the council and to have a vote. Since he lived on the property he saw no need for a spreadsheet to tell him what he could plainly see. His parents lived in town and came to the winery every day. If he successfully lobbied them for his proposals, he now had the winning votes for whatever he wanted.

Questions

1. Is a family council the most effective tool in this instance?

2. How can corporate governance tools best be used in this case?

3. Should pruning be considered? What are the risks?

4. What do you see as the need for improvement here?

Case Study Twelve

Power Struggle with the Board of Directors

Charles (Charley) Ellison and his wife, Nancy, started Ellison's Masonry in 1973. Charley has a very prickly personality: a quick temper and proneness to outbursts of anger. He does not suffer fools well at all and is very vocal when he disagrees or is angry. Charley and Nancy have been working for over 40 years in the business and have grown it to over 450 employees in three states. Sales recently reached 325 million dollars. Charley serves in the dual roles of chairman of the board as well as CEO.

Over the years, with a view to increasing professionalism and effectively managing the firm, they instituted several governance mechanisms, such as a family council, a constitution, and a BOD. The board was created following the sale of 20 percent of the firm to Charley's brother James and his family. James worked for the company for over 30 years and is the main salesperson or bidder. He has an engaging personality, is very likable, and is described as a people person. The company has moved into larger public works projects owing to James's relationships with cities and property developers. James has the title of executive VP.

Through the years, the board has been very useful in financial oversight, making sure the company does not run out of cash through too many acquisitions, and has several board members with contracting experience. Recently, stress has been starting to show in the relationship between Charley and the board. He has been unprofessional at meetings and drags his feet on recommendations made by the board. It has recently approached James about becoming CEO.

Questions

1. Why is the board considering this move?

2. Can the relationship be fixed?

3. What are the risks here?

4. Will the board be successful?

5. What should James do?

6. If you were a family business consultant, what would you advise?

Case Study Thirteen
The Charity Case

Maggie Resson is the granddaughter of Benjamin and Cheryl Resson, the founders of Fast and Quick, a regional hamburger chain that grew to 475 restaurants on the east coast. The chain is headquartered in Boston, where they put their business name on a local stadium. The chain has become very successful, and the family wealth has increased so far as to give several family members, including her grandparents and her parents, billionaire status. The business went public 3 years ago, and the family was able to cash in a portion of their shares for a significant amount of cash. The family decided to open a family office to take care of the business (financial and legal) needs of the family. Maggie worked in the business as a teenager, flipping burgers as most family members did. When she was 32, she married a medical school student, who is now a surgeon in Colorado. Maggie, although a shareholder with significant dividend income, is not able to participate in the family business as many of her cousins and aunts and uncles do. She has decided to get involved under the auspices of the family office and create the philanthropic arm to represent the charitable interests of her family.

Questions

1. What should Maggie do first?

2. How should the philanthropic arm be funded?

3. How should the foundation be led?

4. Will the foundation need a governance structure?

5. What costs are involved?

Case Study Fourteen
Pruning the Family Tree

Praxis Technologies is a 67-year-old firm, with 46 shareholders distributed among seven branches of the family. Started by patriarch Louis Plant and his wife, Stella, the company has grown to be a large player in their industry, with sales approaching $2.7 billion. The Plant's children, Louis Jr., Stella Jr., Martina, Bobby, and Cassandra, all had several children each. There are now 39 grandchildren.

Recently, both Bobby and Cassandra's branches of the family (totaling 13 people) have complained that the company is being mismanaged and that they are unhappy with their dividend payouts. They have been very vocal critics during the family council meetings and at the last two annual shareholder meetings. They have begun lobbying other branches of the family and have begun to get their mother involved (triangulation). The board has decided the company has been adversely affected by their dissonance and the other siblings want to buy out their shares. They offer a price that is fair based on current business conditions and the company cash flow; however, Bobby and Cassandra strongly disagree with the valuation and consider it undervalued and unfair. They have become very hostile and have contacted a lawyer and will be suing the company. They are charging that the board is incompetent and suspect embezzlement is afoot.

Questions

1. How could this have been prevented?

2. If you are a family business consultant, what would you recommend to the family? To Bobby and Cassandra?

3. What are the risks with each of your recommendations?

APPENDIX A

Berkshire Hathaway Inc. Corporate Governance Guidelines

The Board of Directors has adopted the following guidelines to promote the effective governance of the Company. The Board will also review and amend these guidelines as it deems necessary or appropriate.

On behalf of the Company's shareholders, the Board is responsible for overseeing the management of the business and affairs of the Company. The Board acts as the ultimate decision-making body of the Company, except on those matters reserved for or shared with the shareholders of the Company under the laws of Delaware.

Director Qualifications

In choosing directors, the Company seeks individuals who have very high integrity, business savvy, shareholder orientation, and a genuine interest in the Company. The Company is required to elect a majority of directors who are independent. All references to "independent directors" in these guidelines are to directors who are independent according to the criteria for independence established by Section 303A of the New York Stock Exchange Listed Company Manual. The Board does not have limits on the number of terms a director may serve. The Board does not have any retirement or tenure policies that would limit the ability of a director to be nominated for reelection. The Governance, Compensation and Nominating Committee is responsible for nominating directors for election or reelection.

Board Size and Committees

The Board presently has 14 members (four management directors, two non-management but not independent directors and eight independent directors). Under the Bylaws of the Company, the Board has the authority to change its size, and the Board will periodically review its size as appropriate.

The Board has three committees:

Audit; Governance, Compensation and Nominating, and Executive. The Audit, Governance, Compensation and Nominating Committees each consist solely of independent directors. The Board may, from time to time, establish and maintain additional or different committees, as it deems necessary or appropriate.

Voting for Directors

Any nominee for director in an uncontested election (i.e., an election where the number of nominees is not greater than the number of directors to be elected) who receives a greater number of votes "withheld" from his or her election than votes "for" such election shall, promptly following certification of the shareholder vote, offer his or her resignation to the Board for consideration in accordance with the following procedures. All of these procedures shall be completed within 90 days following certification of the shareholder vote.

The Qualified Independent Directors (as defined below) shall evaluate the best interest of the Company and its shareholders and shall decide on behalf of the Board the action to be taken with respect to such offered resignation, which can include: (i) accepting the resignation, (ii) maintaining the director but addressing what the Qualified Independent Directors believe to be the underlying cause of the withheld votes, (iii) resolving that the director will not be re-nominated in the future for election, or (iv) rejecting the resignation.

In reaching their decision, the Qualified Independent Directors shall consider all factors they deem relevant, including: (i) any stated reasons why shareholders withheld votes from such director, (ii) any alternatives for curing the underlying cause of the withheld votes, (iii) the director's tenure, (iv) the director's qualifications, (v) the director's past and expected future contributions to the Company, and (vi) the overall composition of the Board, including whether accepting the resignation would cause the Company to fail to meet any applicable SEC or NYSE requirements.

Following the Board's determination, the Company shall promptly disclose publicly in a document furnished or filed with the SEC the Board's decision of whether or not to accept the resignation offer. The disclosure shall also include an explanation of how the decision was reached, including, if applicable, the reasons for rejecting the offered resignation.

A director who is required to offer his or her resignation in accordance with this Section 3 shall not be present during the deliberations or voting whether to accept his or her resignation or, except as otherwise provided below, a resignation offered by any other director in accordance with this Section 3. Prior to voting, the Qualified Independent Directors will afford the affected director an opportunity to provide any information or statement that he or she deems relevant.

For the purposes of this Section 3, the term *Qualified Independent Directors* means:

A) All directors who (1) are independent directors (as defined in accordance with the NYSE Corporate Governance Rules) and (2) are not required to offer their resignation in accordance with this Section 3.
B) If there are fewer than three independent directors then serving on the Board who are not required to offer their resignations in accordance with this Section 3, then the Qualified Independent Directors shall mean all of the independent directors, and each independent director who is required to offer his or her resignation in accordance with this Section 3 shall recuse himself or herself from the deliberations and voting only with respect to his or her individual offer to resign.

The foregoing procedures will be summarized and disclosed each year in the proxy statement for the Company's annual meeting of shareholders.

Director Responsibilities

The basic responsibility of the directors is to exercise their business judgment to act in what they reasonably believe to be in the best interests of the

Company and its shareholders and to conduct themselves in accordance with their duties of care and loyalty. Directors are expected to attend Board meetings and meetings of the committees on which they serve and to spend the time needed to carry out their responsibilities as directors, including meeting as frequently as necessary to properly discharge those responsibilities. Directors are also expected to review in advance all materials for the meetings of the Board and the Committee(s) on which they serve.

Director Access to Management and Advisors

Each director has full and free access to the officers and employees of the Company and its subsidiaries. The Board and each of its Committees has the authority to hire independent legal, financial, or other advisors as it may deem to be necessary without consulting or obtaining the advance approval of any officer of the Company.

Board Meetings

The Chairman of the Board is responsible for establishing the agenda for each Board meeting. Each director is free to suggest items for inclusion on the agenda and to raise at any Board meeting subjects that are not on the agenda for that meeting. At least once a year, the Board reviews the Company's long-term plans and the principal issues that the Company will face in the future.

Executive Sessions

The non-management directors meet in regularly scheduled executive session (i.e., without directors who are members of management). The independent directors also meet in a separate executive session consisting solely of independent directors at least once a year. The presiding director at each executive session is chosen by the directors present at that meeting.

Director Compensation

Only directors who are neither an employee of the Company or a subsidiary nor a spouse of an employee receive compensation for serving on the Board. Director fees are nominal and are limited to immediate compensation. Changes in the form and amount of director compensation are determined by the full Board, taking into consideration the Company's policy that the fees should be of no consequence to any director serving the Company. The Board critically reviews any amounts that a director might receive directly or indirectly from the Company, as well as any charitable contributions the Company may make to organizations with which a director is affiliated, in determining whether a director is independent. The Company does not purchase director's and officer's liability insurance for its directors or officers.

Orientation and Continuing Education

All new directors receive an orientation from the Chief Executive Officer and are expected to maintain the necessary level of expertise to perform his or her responsibilities as a director. The Company does not maintain any formal orientation or continuing education programs.

Management Succession

Assuring that the Company has the appropriate successor to the current Chief Executive Officer in the event of his death or disability is one of the Board's primary responsibilities. The Company does not anticipate that the Chief Executive Officer will retire other than due to disability. The Chief Executive Officer reports annually to the Board on executive management succession planning and makes available, on a continuing basis, his recommendation on succession in the event he was disabled. The Board and the committees of non-management directors and independent directors regularly review succession planning and the strengths and weaknesses of certain individuals currently employed by the Company who could succeed the Chief Executive Officer in the event of his death or disability.

The Governance, Compensation and Nominating Committee is responsible for evaluation of the performance of the Company's Chief Executive Officer and setting his compensation.

Annual Performance Evaluation

The Governance, Compensation and Nominating Committee conducts an annual evaluation to determine whether the Board and its committees are functioning effectively and reports its conclusions to the Board. Each of the Audit Committee and the Governance, Compensation and Nominating Committee separately conducts an annual evaluation of its performance relative to the requirements of its Charter and reports its conclusions to the Board. The Board annually conducts a self-evaluation of its performance based in part on the reports of these two Committees.

Public Disclosure of Corporate Governance Policies

The Company posts on its website copies of the current version of these guidelines, the Company's Code of Business Conduct and Ethics and the charters of the Audit Committee and the Governance, Compensation and Nominating Committee of the Board, and discloses in its annual report that such information is available on its website or in print to any shareholder that requests it.

Source: BerkshireHathaway.com

APPENDIX B

Chick-fil-A (CFA) Statement of California Transparency in Supply Chains Act of 2010

In accordance with the California Transparency in Supply Chains Act of 2010, CFA makes the following disclosures:

CFA requires its vendors to certify that their business practices are lawful, ethical and in compliance with the principles set forth in CFA's Vendor Code of Conduct (including those provisions relating to human trafficking and slavery), and that they take steps to ensure the same of their own supply chains. To ensure accountability, CFA reserves the right to terminate its business relationship with any vendor who fails to provide such certifications or whose business practices, or the business practices of its own suppliers and subcontractors, are not lawful, ethical and in compliance with the principles set forth in CFA's Vendor Code of Conduct. CFA also reserves the right to terminate its business relationship with vendors who fail to provide written confirmation to CFA that they have a program in place to monitor their suppliers and subcontractors for compliance with law, good ethics, and the principles set forth in CFA's Vendor Code of Conduct. CFA reserves the right to conduct verification and audits (including third-party verification and audits) of its suppliers regarding human trafficking and slavery. CFA has conducted general audits of certain of its suppliers and has not observed violations with respect to human trafficking or slavery issues. CFA is currently considering whether and how to best use third-party supply chain verification and independent unannounced audits with its suppliers. CFA provides company employees and management who have direct responsibility for supply chain management with training on CFA's business practices, vendor requirements, and CFA's Vendor Code of Conduct, including those provisions relating to mitigating risks of human trafficking and slavery. Employees and management failing to meet CFA standards regarding slavery and trafficking are subject to disciplinary action. https://www.chick-fil-a.com/Legal

APPENDIX C

International Finance Corporation Definition of an Independent Director

"Independent Director" means a Director who has no direct or indirect material relationship with the Company other than membership on the Board and who:

A) is not, and has not been in the past 5 years, employed by the Company or its Affiliates;

B) does not have, and has not had in the past 5 years, a business relationship with, and does not hold a material interest in, the Company or its Affiliates (either directly or as a partner or shareholder (other than to the extent to which shares are held by such Director pursuant to a requirement of Applicable Law in the Country relating to directors generally), and is not a partner, shareholder, director, officer or senior employee of a Person that has or had such a relationship);

C) is not affiliated with any nonprofit organization that receives significant funding from the Company or its Affiliates;

D) does not receive and has not received in the past 5 years, any additional remuneration from the Company or its Affiliates other than his or her director's fee and such director's fee does not constitute a significant portion of his or her annual income;

E) does not participate in any share option [scheme]/[plan] or pension [scheme]/[plan] of the Company or any of its Affiliates;

F) is not employed as an executive officer of another company where any of the Company's executives serve on that company's board of directors;

G) is not, nor has been at any time during the past 5 years, affiliated with or employed by a present or former auditor of the Company or any of its Affiliates;

H) is not a member of the immediate family (and is not the executor, administrator or personal representative of any such Person who is deceased or legally incompetent) of any individual who would not meet any of the tests set out in (a) to (g) (were he or she a director of the Company);

I) is identified in the annual report of the Company distributed to the shareholders of the Company as an independent director; and

J) has not served on the Board for more than 10 years.

For purposes of this definition, "material interest" shall mean a direct or indirect ownership of [voting] shares representing at least 2 percent of the outstanding [voting power] or equity of the Company or any of its Affiliates.

Family Business Resources

The FFI is the premiere international body for research and advising in the family business and family wealth fields.

The International Family Enterprise Research Academy (IFERA)
IFERA is devoted to research, theory, and practice of family business with an emphasis on scholarship.

Family Business Magazine
A general readership publication designed for family business members. https://www.familybusinessmagazine.com/

The Family Business Network (FBN)
The FBN is a not-for-profit international network operated by family businesses, for family businesses, with the goal of strengthening family business success over generations. They have thousands of family business members all over the world.

Family Enterprise USA (FEUSA)
FEUSA is a membership advocacy group whose primary purpose is to increase public awareness of the importance of family business.

United States Association of Small Business and Entrepreneurship (USASBE)
USASBE includes a family business special interest group within this organization, the largest entrepreneurial association in the United States.

The Institute for Family Business (IFB)
The IFB is an independent nonprofit organization that supports family business in the United Kingdom through research, education, and policy advocacy (see http://www.ifb.org.uk).

Tharawat Family Business Forum
The Tharawat Family Business Forum is an Arab family business network established in 2007. It publishes *Tharawat Magazine*.

The Family Wealth Alliance specializes in the businesses that target family firms, including family offices and wealth management professionals. https://www.familywealthalliance.com/cpages/about

Glossary

agency theory. This theoretical construct believes that people will act in their own self-interest.

AGM (annual general meeting or annual shareholders meeting). This is the annual meeting of all the owners (stockholders or shareholders) of the firm.

altruism. Unselfish concern for the welfare of others at the expense of oneself. Families can make business decisions that hurt the business, such as avoiding layoffs in a downturn or keeping a long-term yet unproductive employee.

audit committee. This is a subcommittee made up of members of the BOD. The audit committee audits (or reviews) the financial reports.

board of advisors. This board is an informal group that offers advice and recommendations to the business. The family business is not required to institute their recommendations.

board of directors. The board of directors (BOD) is a governance mechanism designed to provide open communication, improved decision making, and increased levels of knowledge and experience in offering advice and instructions to the TMT. The board provides oversight of the organization. Board members are elected, have liability, and are compensated for their contributions.

chairman of the board. This is the person who is elected to chair or lead the BOD.

chief executive officer. This is an officer of the corporation, the leader of the TMT and responsible for the team with day-to-day management responsibility for running the business. The CEO answers to the BOD.

commitment. This is the desire of an employee or family member to continue with the firm.

compensation committee. This is a subcommittee made up of members of the BOD. It conducts benchmark research for market rate comparables and recommends employment compensation rates to the BOD.

competitive advantage. A competitive advantage exists when one company has something rare and hard to copy that places competitors at a disadvantage.

conflict. This means to be in serious and direct opposition to another's ideas, viewpoints, plans, and strategy. Conflict can extend to the point of violent disagreement. When this occurs interpersonally, especially among family members, it has a negative impact on the family business. Conversely, conflict can be positive if all sides are able to share freely and debate over the process of how work should be done (called task conflict). In this manner, good decisions can be made, and work is performed efficiently.

conflict of interest. In a family business, this occurs when personal interests conflict with business interests.

control. This is used when discussing large companies, often with outside share-holders. The family may have enough ownership to exercise a high level of input on the strategic direction of the firm.

corporate social responsibility (CSR). Corporate and governance activists are demanding that corporations be responsible in their actions toward society (stakeholders).

cousin consortium. It is made up of third-generation members of the family.

culture. This is a company's unique set of values, norms, beliefs, history, and experiences that make up the unique character of the organization. In a family business with a "positive" culture, the family members and employees have a shared system of beliefs, attitudes, and norms of behavior. It can be a source of tremendous competitive advantage. Conversely, in a business with a "negative" organizational culture, the employees do not share a similar value system, owners and managers may be at odds with employees, and there are no norms to guide decisions.

director. A director is an elected member of the BOD.

dual class shares. These shares allow for more votes than regular shares of common stock. They are also referred to as super shares. Families can control a corporation with dual classes of stock that do not match their ownership rights.

dual roles. This occurs when one person holds two roles in an organization, such as the chairman of the BOD and the chief executive officer roles simultaneously. It is a common yet controversial practice with overtones of conflicts of interest.

entrepreneur. This is the original creator or founder of the firm. Usually, one person can sometimes be a small partnership.

entrepreneurial orientation. This is the likelihood that the family will continue to be entrepreneurial through the generations.

estate planning. This refers to the proactive discussion and planning for a person's disposition of property, possessions, and capital. It is usually purposefully and proactively structured to minimize taxes and maximize generational wealth.

explicit knowledge. This type of knowledge is clear and obvious. It is gained by education and reading and expressed by words, numbers, and codes. It is the opposite of tacit knowledge.

family. This most commonly refers to a nuclear family of blood relatives, such as a father, a mother, and their offspring. In family business terms, it can refer to extended family members and in-laws. The individuals are committed to mutual growth and development. They share a family history together and have strong bonds.

familiness. A term created to describe the interplay between the family and the business, it includes the various forms of capital, such as human, social, financial, and physical, that are unique to the family business.

family business. There is not one well-accepted definition of family business. The most common definition is where the family, consisting of more than one family member, owns a significant amount of the firm and influences the strategy of the business by the control of shares or votes.

family constitution. This is a tool of governance and refers to a written document the family creates and agrees to. It lists numerous items such as who can own stock and the policy for how the company terminates a family member.

family controlled. This is, typically, a larger firm that has gone public (sold shares to the public), where the family has either a simple majority of the stock or a dual class type of share, in which the family has more votes per share than common stockholders, thereby having control of the business. It is common in S&P 500 family firms.

family council. This is a more formal governance mechanism than a family meeting. It has an agenda, decisions are made by voting, and it is often run by an outside facilitator. In large firms, members are elected. The council interacts with the board and informs them of the family's decisions and issues of importance.

family employees. These are employees of the business who are also members of the owning family.

family meeting. This is an informal meeting of the family to provide updates to family members.

family office. This is a group of service professionals who manage the family wealth as well as providing accountancy and legal services, specifically for the family. Usually the family charitable foundations are housed in the family office.

family roles. Familial roles are generally assigned to us early in life. For example, the youngest member of the family is the baby, the older child has extra responsibilities, and there may be the black sheep of the family. It can be difficult for other family members to see the person as anything different.

founder. The original entrepreneur who started the business, the founder, also referred to as the controlling owner.

generation one (Gen 1). This is the first generation of family ownership, usually the entrepreneur or original founder, often referred to as the controlling owner.

generation two (Gen 2). This generation consists of the sons and daughters of the founder. The siblings are referred to as a sibling partnership.

generation three (Gen 3). This generation is becoming larger, with many cousins involved and different branches of the family. It is referred to as a cousin's consortium.

governance. These comprise formal measures of control instituted for effective management of the firm. Governance items include boards of directors, the family constitution, the family council, etc. There are three parts to effective family business governance—governance of the family, the business, and ownership.

human capital. This is a measure of the economic value of the employee or employees.

independence. In terms of board members, independence is important among many of the directors of the board to increase ideas, communication, and question decisions among what may be a family-controlled firm. It is also referred to as outsiders and means the opposite of insiders.

insiders. It refers to people who are family members or those close to the family. Their loyalty usually lies with the family. It may also refer to employees of the firm.

legacy. This is what the founder leaves behind. In the case of a family business, this may be a successful firm and the norms, mission, and vision handed down through the generations.

management. This is the administration, organization, and control of the business. Proper management is necessary for success.

mission statement. This is a statement that defines the purpose, duty, objective, or task of the family business.

nepotism. This refers to preferential treatment of family members in regard to employment, promotions, and compensation.

nomination committee of the board of directors. This is a subcommittee made up of members of the BOD.

nonemployed family members. These are family members who are not employed at the business. They may be owners or nonowners.

nonfamily employees. These are employees who are not members of the owning family. They are considered outsiders.

outsiders. This refers to those people outside of the family and the business. An example would be a nonfamily member director with no ties to the family or the company.

owners. People or families that hold ownership shares (stock) in the business.

pruning. To avoid having too many family employees or to keep the business in only one branch of the family, other family members may be bought out or encouraged to start a separate business.

resource-based view (RBV). This view states that a family firm has a sustainable competitive advantage based on the unique capabilities, resources, and relationships that nonfamily firms do not have and cannot develop.

shareholder assembly. This is a small group of owners of the business. It differs from the family council in that some may be nonfamily members. They meet several times a year, their main purpose being to oversee the financial liquidity and stability of the business.

sibling rivalry. As the children grow, they may engage in competitive or aggressive behavior aimed at securing parental love and affection. This behavior can exhibit itself when siblings try to break out of their family roles, with the conflict becoming problematic in the family firm.

social capital. The resources (e.g., ideas, information, money, and trust) that an individual can access through their social network. A high level of earned social capital is thought to be one reason behind a family firm's competitive advantage.

social identity theory. Developed by social psychologists, it postulates that individuals behave in certain and often predictable ways as members of a group such as a family business, to which they have loyalty.

social network. This is a social structure consisting of individuals or organizations connected by ties such as a relationship, link, or bond.

socioemotional wealth. This is a popular family business theory that discusses the importance of the emotional component within the family. The value that a family gets from their ownership of the firm is not just monetary but includes family pride and their standing in the community.

stockholders (or shareholders). These are people or organizations that own shares of stock in the company.

stakeholder. A stakeholder is anyone or any organization that has a stake in the family business (will be affected by its success or failure). Stakeholders include the employees, the community, the customers, the suppliers, etc.

stakeholder theory. Stakeholder theory believes that all stakeholders should be considered and not just the shareholders of a firm.

strategic planning. A process used to define the company objectives, assess internal and external situations, formulate a strategy, implement the strategy, evaluate the strategy,, and make necessary adjustments.

succession. This refers to the transfer of ownership or leadership from one generation to another and is likely the most problematic issue in a family business.

system. This is a combination of related individual parts organized into a whole. A family business is a complex system with three subsystems—the family, the business, and the ownership of the business.

tacit knowledge. This type of knowledge is gained by being with and around other people; it is a sum of experiences, requiring joint or shared activities to develop. It is implicit, unspoken, and gained by observation and is the opposite of explicit knowledge.

the three-circle model (systems approach). This theoretical approach places people in three overlapping circles—ownership, business, and family. The model can be used to understand the complex and different roles and various constituencies by one's placement within the model.

top management team (TMT). This is the C-level team that runs the day-to-day business operations, and it consists of the CEO, the COO, the CFO, etc.

transparency. Corporate governance advocates are demanding greater corporate transparency (better reports, open communication, ability to ask questions).

triangulation. This is a negative technique used to elicit support from one family member against another. The person being asked for support is placed in the middle of two conflicting family members.

trust. In family businesses, trust is a critical component and is necessary in the creation of a competitive advantage. Agency costs are reduced because of high levels of trust. Conversely, when a family is low on trust, dysfunction results.

values. These are the principles, standards, and norms to which the business aspires. In a family business, the values are accepted by the group and are often passed down to successive generations.

vision. The long-term goals of the family business, usually expressed in a vision statement.

References

Alderson, K. 2009. *Exploring the Complexities of Family Business Decision Making: How the Second Generation Makes Decisions.* Ann Arbor, MI: UMI.

Alderson, K. 2015. "Conflict Management and Resolution in the Family Owned Business: A Practitioner Focused Review." *Journal of Family Business Management* 5, no. 2, pp. 140–56.

Alderson, K. 2018. *Understanding the Family Business: Exploring the Differences Between Family and Non-Family Owned Businesses.* 2nd ed. New York, NY: Business Expert Press.

Anderson, R., and D. Reeb. 2003. "Founding Family Ownership and Firm Performance: Evidence from the S&P 500." *Journal of Finance* 58, pp. 1301–1328.

Aronoff, C.E., and J.H. Astrachan. 1996. "How to Make Better Decisions." *Nations Business* 84, no. 1, p. 39.

Astrachan, J.H., and M.C. Shanker. 2003. "Family Businesses' Contribution to the US Economy: A Closer Look." *Family Business Review* 16, pp. 211–219

Automotive News. 2013. "Bill Ford Nearly Doubles Stake in Fords Super Voting Shares." Retrieved April, 24, 2018 from: http://www.autonews.com/article/20130626/OEM02/130629906/bill-ford-nearly-doubles-stake-in-fords-supervoting-shares.

Bacardi Limited. 2018. "Statement of Corporate Responsibility." Retrieved May 24, 2018 from: https://www.bacardilimited.com/corporate-responsibility/at-bacardi-limited/

Barney, J.B. 1991. "Firm Resources and Sustained Competitive Advantage." *Journal of Management* 17, pp. 99–120.

Berkshire Hathaway Inc. 2018. "Corporate Governance Guidelines." Retrieved November 1, 2018 from: http://berkshirehathaway.com/govern/corpgov.pdf

Berkshire Hathaway Inc. 2018. "Governance, Compensation and Nominating Committee Charter." Retrieved November 1, 2018 from: http://berkshirehathaway.com/govern/comp.pdf

Björnberg, Å., H.-P. Elstrodt, and V. Pandit. 2015. "Joining the Family Business: An Emerging Opportunity for Investors." *McKinsey on Investing* 2, pp. 22–26.

Block, J. 2010. "Family Management, Family Ownership, and Downsizing: Evidence from S&P 500 Firms." *Family Business Review* 23, no. 2, pp. 109–130.

Bloomberg.com. 2018. "Company Overview of Herschend Family Entertainment Corporation." https://www.bloomberg.com/research/stocks/private/board.asp?privcapId=1022128

Blumentritt, T., Keyt, A., and Astrachan, J. 2007. "Creating an Environment for Successful Nonfamily CEOs: An Exploratory Study of Good Principles." *Family Business Review* 20, pp. 321–355.

Braun, M., and A. Sharma. 2007. "Should the CEO Also be Chair of the Board? An Empirical Examination of Family-Controlled Public Firms." *Family Business Review* 20, no. 2, pp. 111–126

Breeze, B. 2009. Natural philanthropists: findings of the family business philanthropy and social responsibility inquiry. Project report. Canterbury, UK: Institute for Family Business. University of Kent. https://kar.kent. ac.uk/37241/

Brenes, E. R., K. Madrigal, and B. Requena. 2009. "Corporate Governance and the Family Business Performance." *Journal of Business Research* 64, no. 3, pp. 280–285.

Buffet, W. 2014. "Annual Letter to Shareholders, Berkshire Hathaway." http://www.berkshirehathaway.com/letters/2014ltr.pdf

Cadbury, S.A. 1999. "What are the Trends in Corporate Governance? How Will They Impact Your Company?" *Long Range Planning* 32, no. 1, pp. 12–19.

Cadbury, S.A. 2000. *Family Firms and their Governance: Creating Tomorrow's Company from Today's.* Zurich, Switzerland: Egon Zehnder International.

Carney, M. 2005. "Corporate Governance and Competitive Advantage in Family-Controlled Firms." *Entrepreneurship Theory and Practice* 29, pp. 249–265.

Carr, D. 2012. "The Cozy Compliance of the NewsCorp Board," *The New York Times.* NYTimes.com

Colli, A., P. Fernandez-Perez, and M. Rose. 2003. "National Determinants of Family Firm Development: Family Firms in Britain, Spain and Italy in the 19th and 20th Centuries." *Enterprise and Society* 4, no. 1, pp. 28–65.

Colquitt, J.A., J.A. LePine, and M.J. Wesson. 2018. *Organizational Behavior: Improving Performance and Commitment in the Workplace.* 6th ed. New York, NY: McGraw-Hill.

Cope, N. April 16, 1997. "Clark Family in Sell Off Bonanza," *The Independent.* London, UK.

Corbetta, G., and C. Salvato. 2004. "The Board of Directors in Family Firms: One Size Fits All?" *Family Business Review* 17, no. 2, pp. 119–134.

Charkham, J.P., and A. Simpson. 1999. *Fair Shares.* Oxford, UK: Clarendon.

Chick-fil-a.com. n.d. "Statement of California Transparency in Supply Chains Act of 2010." Retrieved November 2, 2018 from: Chick-filA.com

Chrisman, J.J., J.H. Chua, and L. Steier. 2005. "Sources and Consequences of Distinctive Familiness: An Introduction." *Entrepreneurship Theory and Practice* 29, pp. 237–247.

Chrisman, J.J., J.H. Chua, and P. Sharma. 2003. *Current trends and future directions in family business management studies: Toward a theory of the family firm.* Coleman White Paper Series. Kent, OH: Coleman Foundation and U.S. Association of Small Business and Entrepreneurship.

Chua, J. H., J.J. Chrisman, and P. Sharma. Summer, 1999. "Defining the Family Business by Behavior." *Entrepreneurship Theory and Practice* 23, no. 4, pp. 19–39.

Crittenden, W.F., N. Athanassiou, and L. Kelly. 2000. "Founder Centrality and Strategic Behavior in the Family Owned Firm." *Entrepreneurship Theory and Practice* 25, no. 2, pp. 27–42.

CS Family 1000. 2017. "Credit Suisse Research Institute." https://credit-suisse.com/corporate/en/research/research-institute/publications.html

Cunningham. 2014. "Liquidity and Control at Buffet's Berkshire Hathaway," *Concurring Opinions.* https://concurringopinions.com/archives/2014/02/calculating-berkshire-hathaways-voting-interest-and-economic-power.html

Davis, J.H., F.D. Schoorman, and L. Donaldson. 1997. "Toward a Stewardship Theory of Management." *Academy of Management Review* 22, pp. 20–47.

Davis, P.S., and P.D. Harveston. 1999. "In the Founder's Shadow: Conflict in the Family Firm." *Family Business Review* 12, pp. 311–323.

Dyck, B., and D. Schroeder. 2005. "Management, Theology and Moral Points of View." *Journal of Management Studies* 42, no. 4, pp. 705–735.

Eckrich, C.J., and S.L. McClure. 2012. *The Family Council Handbook.* New York, NY: Palgrave MacMillan.

Eddleston, K.A., and F.W. Kellermanns. 2007. "Destructive and productive family relationships: A stewardship theory perspective." *Journal of Business Venturing* 22, no. 4, pp. 545–565.

Eddleston, K.A., J.J. Chrisman, L.P. Steier, and J.H. Chua. 2010. "Governance and Trust in Family Firms: An Introduction." *Entrepreneurship Theory and Practice* 34, no. 6, pp. 1042–1056.

Eddleston, K.A., R.F. Otondo, and F.W. Kellermanns. 2008. "Conflict, Participative Decision-Making, and Generational Ownership Dispersion: A Multilevel Analysis." *Journal of Small Business Management* 46, pp. 456–484.

Edelman Trust Barometer. 2017. "Special Report: Family Business." https://edelman.com/trust2017/family-business-trust/

Eisenhardt, K. 1989. "Agency Theory: An Assessment Review." *Academy of Management Review* 14, no. 1, pp. 57–74.

Eisenhardt, K., J. Kahwajy, and L. Bourgeois. 1997. "How Management Teams Can Have a Good Fight." *Harvard Business Review* 75, no. 4, pp. 77–85.

Elcompanies.com. 2018. "Estee Lauder Board of Directors." https://www.elcompanies.com/who-we-are/leadership/board-of-directors

EY. 2015. "Women in Leadership: The Family Business Advantage," 2018. *Ernst & Young.* Retrieved July 8, 2018 from: https://www.ey.com/Publication/vwLUAssets/ey-women-in-leadership-the-family-business-advantage/$FILE/ey-women-in-leadership-the-family-business-advantage.pdf

Fama, E.F., and M.C. Jensen. June, 1998. "Separation of Ownership and Control." *Journal of Law and Economics* 26.

Feltham, T.S., G. Feltham, and J.J. Barnett. 2005. "The Dependence of Family Businesses on a Single Decision Maker." *Journal of Small Business Management* 43, no. 1, pp. 1–15.

FFI Practitioner. June 12, 2018. "The Future of the Three-Circle Model: An Interview with John Davis and Pramadita Sharma." https://ffipractitioner.org/the-future-of-the-three-circle-model-a-conversation-between-pramodita-sharma-and-john-davis/

Ford.com. 2018. "Ford Motor Company Board of Directors." https://media.ford.com/content/fordmedia/fna/us/en/people.filter.members-of-the-board.0.10.html

Freeman, R.E. 1984. *Strategic Management: A Stakeholder Approach. The Pitman Series in Business and Public Policy.* New York, NY: Harper Collins College Division.

Friedman, M. September 13, 1970. "The Social Responsibility of Business Is to Increase Its Profits." *New York Times Magazine*, 2.

Gersick, K.E., J.A. Davis, M.M. Hampton, and I. Lansberg. 1997. *Generation to Generation: Life Cycles of the Family Business.* Boston, MA: Harvard Business School Press.

Gomez-Mejia, L.R., C. Cruz, P. Berrone, and J. De Castro. 2011. "The Bind That Ties: Socioemotional Wealth Preservation in Family Firms." *Academy of Management Annals* 5, pp. 653–707.

Gomez-Mejia, L.R., M. Nunez-Nickel, and I. Guttierez. 2001. "The Role of Family Ties in Agency Contracts." *Academy of Management Journal* 44, no. 1, pp. 1–95.

Gomez-Mejia, L.R., K. Haynes, M. Nunez-Nickel, K.J. Jacobson, and J. Mayonna-Fuentes. 2007. "Socioemotional Wealth and Business Risks in Family Controlled Firms: Evidence from Spanish Olive Oil Mills." *Administrative Science Quarterly* 52, no. 1, pp. 106–137.

Gordon, G., and N. Nicholson. 2008. *Family Wars: Stories and Insights from Famous Family Business Feuds.* London, UK: Kogan Page.

Habbershon, T.G., and M.L. Williams. 1999. "A Resource-Based Framework for Assessing the Strategic Advantages of Family Firms." *Family Business Review* 12, pp. 1–25.

Habbershon, T.G., M. Williams, and I.C. MacMillan. 2003. "A Unified Systems Perspective of Family Firm Performance." *Journal of Business Venturing* 18, pp. 451–465.

Hallmark.com. 2018. *Culture.* https://corporate.hallmark.com/culture/hallmark-family/vision-beliefs-values/

Huse, M., and H. Landström. 2002. *Teaching Corporate Governance: Challenges for Research and Practice.* Conference Presentation, EURAM Meeting.

Ibrahim, N.A., J.P. Angelides and F. Parsa. 2008. "Strategic Management of Family Businesses: Current Findings and Directions for Future Research." *International Journal of Management* 25, no. 1, pp. 95–110.

IFC, International Finance Corporation. 2008. *Family Business Governance Handbook*, retrieved August 11, 2018 from: https://www.ifc.org/wps/wcm/connect/159c9c0048582f6883f9ebfc046daa89/FB_English_final_2008.pdf?MOD=AJPERES

Institute of Directors in Southern Africa. 2016. "King IV, report on corporate governance for South Africa." https://c.ymcdn.com/sites/www.iodsa.co.za/resource/resmgr/king_iv/King_IV_Report/IoDSA_King_IV_Report_-_WebVe.pdf

JD Supra. December 19, 2011. "California Transparency in Supply Chains Act Takes Effect January 1, 2012," *Corporate Law Report.* http://corporatelaw.jdsupra.com/post/california-transparency-in-supply-chains-takes-effect

Jensen, M.C. 1998. "Self-Interest, Altruism, Incentives, and Agency." In *Foundations of Organizational Strategy,* ed. M.C. Jensen. Cambridge, MA: Harvard Business School Press, pp. 48–62.

Jensen, M.C., and W.H. Meckling. 1976. "Theory of the Firm: Managerial Behavior, Agency Costs and Capital Structure." *Journal of Financial Economics* 3, pp. 305–360.

Kachaner, N., G. Stalk, and A. Bloch. November 2012. "What You Can Learn from Family Business." *Harvard Business Review* 90, no. 11, pp. 103–106.

Kellermanns, F.W., and K.A. Eddleston. 2004. "Feuding Families: When Conflict Does a Family Firm Good." *Entrepreneurship Theory and Practice* 28, pp. 209–228.

Kelly, L.M., N. Athanassiou, and W.F. Crittenden. 2000. "Founder Centrality and Strategic Behavior in the Family Owned Firm." *Entrepreneurship Theory and Practice* 25, pp. 27–42.

Kets de Vries, M.F.R. 1993. "The Dynamics of Family Controlled Firms: The Good and Bad News." *Organizational Dynamics* 21, no. 3, pp. 59–71.

Koberle-Schmid, A., D. Kenyon-Rouvinez, and E.J. Poza. 2014. *Governance in Family Firms: Maximising Economic and Emotional Success.* New York, NY: Palgrave MacMillan.

Lee, J. 2006. "Family firm performance: Further evidence." *Family Business Review,* 19, no. 2, pp.103–114.

Martin, G. 2014. "La Vita Beretta: At Home in Italy with the First Family of Firearms," *Forbes Life.* https://www.forbes.com/sites/forbeslifestyle/2014/09/10/inside-the-beretta-empire-a-fashion-line-hunting-lodges-and-an-italian-villa/#aabbc673014b

MassMutual Financial Group/Raymond Institute. 2002. *American family business survey*. Retrieved March 20, 2017, from http://kennesaw.edu/fec/DMD9500R.pdf

MassMutual Financial Group. 2007. *American family business survey*. Retrieved July 10, 2018 from https://www.massmutual.com/mmfg/pdf/afbs.pdf

McCann, G. 2007. *When Your Parents Sign the Paychecks: Finding Career Success Inside or Outside the Family Business*. Indianapolis, IN: Jist Works.

McConaughy, D.L., C.H. Matthews, and A.S. Fialko. 2001. "Founding Family Controlled Firms: Performance, Risk, and Value." *Journal of Small Business Management* 39, no. 1, pp. 31–49.

McKinsey Global Institute. 2014. *Perspectives on Founder and Family-Owned Businesses*. New York, NY: McKinsey & Company.

McKinsey Global Institute. 2015. *Playing to Win: The New Global Competition for Corporate Profits*. New York, NY: McKinsey & Company.

McKinsey & Company. July, 2002. "Global Investor Opinion Survey on Corporate Governance, Key Findings." http://www.eiod.org/uploads/publications/pdf/ii-rp-4-1.pdf

Miller, D., and I. Le Breton-Miller. 2003. "Challenge Versus Advantage in Family Business." *Strategic Organization* 1, no. 1, pp. 127–134.

Miller, D., and I. Le Bretton-Miller. 2005. *Managing for the Long Run: Lessons in Competitive Advantage from Great Family Businesses*. Boston, MA: Harvard Business School Publishing.

Miller, D., and I. Le Breton-Miller. 2006. "Family Governance and Firm Performance: Agency, Stewardship, and Capabilities." *Family Business Review* 19, pp. 73–87.

Miller, D., I. Le Bretton-Miller, and R.H. Lester. 2011. "Family and Lone Founder Ownership and Strategic Behaviour: Social Context, Identity, and Institutional Logics." *Journal of Management Studies* 48, no. 1, pp. 1–25.

Montemerlo, D., and J.L. Ward. 2011. *The Family Constitution*. New York, NY: Palgrave Macmillan.

Morck, R., and B. Yeung. 2003. "Agency Problems in Large Family Business Groups." *Entrepreneurship Theory and Practice* 27, pp. 367–82.

Morck, R., D. Wolfenzon, and B. Yeung. 2005. "Corporate Governance, Economic Entrenchment, and Growth." *Journal of Economic Literature* 43, no. 3, pp. 577–720.

Muller, J. December 2, 2010. "Ford Family's Stake is Smaller, but They're Richer and Still Firmly in Control," *Forbes*. https://www.forbes.com/sites/joannmuller/2010/12/02/ford-familys-stake-is-smaller-but-theyre-richer-and-remain-firmly-in-control/#5f7176342174

Murray, B., K. Gersick, and I. Lansberg. 2001/2002. "From Back Office to Executive Suite—The Evolving Role of the Family Office." *Private Wealth Management,* pp. 111–114. Retrieved February 21, 2018 from: https://www.lgassoc.com/writing/2017/12/6/from-back-office-to-executive-suite-the-evolving-role-of-the-family-office

Mustakallio, M.A., and E. Autio. 2001. "Effects of Formal and Social Controls on Strategic Decision Making in Family Firms." In *The Role of Family in Family Business*, eds. G. Corbetta, and D. Montemerlo. Milan, Italy: EGEA, pp. 89–107.

Mustakillio, M., E. Autio, and S.A. Zahra. 2002. "Relational and Contractual Governance in Family Firms: Effects on Strategic Decision Making." *Family Business Review* XV, no. 3, pp. 205–222.

Newscorp.com. 2018. "Newscorp Board of Directors." https://newscorp.com/corporate-governance/board-of-director

Niehm, L., J. Swinney, and N.J. Miller. 2008. "Community Social Responsibility and its Consequences for Family Business Performance." *Journal of Small Business Management* 46, no. 3, pp. 331–50.

OECD, Organization for Economic Co-operation and Development. 2007. "Governance Challenges for Family Owned Businesses (Chapter Five)." In *Practical Guide to Corporate Governance*. https://www.oecd.org/daf/ca/corporategovernanceprinciples/43654301.pdf

O'Kane, S. September 29, 2018. "Elon Musk Forced to Step Down as Chairman of Tesla, Remains CEO," *The Verge*. https://www.theverge.com/2018/9/29/17918252/elon-musk-tesla-sec-securities-fraud-lawsuit-settlement-fine-penalty

Pearl, J.A. Spring, 2010. "Pruning the Family Tree." *Family Business Magazine* 21, no. 2, pp. 61–64.

Pindado, J., and I. Requejo. 2015. "Family Business Performance from a Governance Perspective: A Review of Empirical Research." *International Journal of Management Reviews* 17, no. 3, pp. 279–311.

Poza, E.J., and M.S. Daugherty. 2014. *Family Business*. 4th ed. New York, NY: Cengage.

PWC. 2014. "What Is a Board's Role in a Family Business?" *Family Business Corporate Governance Series. PWC*. Retrieved November 22, 2018 from: https://www.google.com/search?q=%3A+PwC+Mod_1+Role+of+CG+in+Private+Family+Companies_FINAL-1.pdf&ie=utf-8&oe=utf-8&client=firefox-b-1-ab

PWC. 2016. "2016 Family Business Survey." https://www.pwc.com/gx/en/services/family-business/family-business-survey-2016.html

Revilla, A.J., A. Perez-Luno, and M.J. Nieto. 2016. "Does Family Involvement in Management Reduce the Risk of Business Failure? The Moderating Role of Entrepreneurial Orientation." *Family Business Review* 29, no. 4, pp. 365–79.

Rhodes, K., and D. Lansky. 2013. *Managing Conflict in the Family Business*. New York, NY: Palgrave Macmillan.

Schulze, W.S., M.H. Lubatkin, R.N. Dino, and A.K. Buchholtz. 2001. "Agency Relationships in Family Firms: Theory and Evidence." *Organization Science* 12, no. 2, pp. 99–116.

Schwartz, M., and L. Barnes. 1991. "Outside Boards and Family Businesses: Another Look." *Family Business Review* 4, no. 3, pp. 269–285.

SC Johnson.com. n.d.-a. "This We Believe: Our Company Values Have Guided SC Johnson for Five Generations." https://www.scjohnson.com/en/a-family-company/what-it-means-to-be-a-family-company/this-we-believe-our-company-values-have-guided-sc-johnson-for-five-generations.

SC Johnson.com. n.d.-b. "Commitment to Transparency." https://www.scjohnson.com/en/our-purpose/commitment-to-transparency/ingredient-transparency-sc-johnson-offers-product-ingredient-lists-so-you-can-make-choices

Sharma, P., J.J. Chrisman, and J.H. Chua. 1996. *A Review and Annotated Bibliography of Family Business Studies*. Boston, MA: Kluwer Academic.

Shevory, K. 2007. "For Tabasco Sauce-Making Family, No Bland Plans," *The New York Times*.

Siler, J.F. 2007. *The House of Mondavi: The Rise and Fall of an American Wine Dynasty*. New York, NY: Gotham.

Smit, B. 2008. *Sneaker Wars: The Enemy Brothers Who Founded Adidas and Puma and the Family Feud That Forever Changed the Business of Sports*. New York, NY: Harper-Collins.

Steier, L. 2001. "Family Firms, Plural Forms of Governance, and the Evolving Role of Trust." *Family Business Review* 14, no. 4, pp. 353–67.

Stroh, F. 2016. *Beer Money: A Memoir of Privilege and Loss*. New York, NY: Harper.

Susanto, A.B., and P. Susanto. 2013. *The Dragon Network: Inside Stories of the Most Successful Chinese Family Businesses*. New York, NY: Bloomberg Press.

Tabasco.com. 2018. "McIlhenny Corporation History." https://www.tabasco.com/tabasco-history/

Tagiuri, R. and J. Davis. 1996. "Bivalent Attributes of the Family Firm." *Family Business Review* 9, no. 2, pp. 199–208.

Template.net. 2018. "Annual Meeting Agenda." https://www.template.net/business/agenda-templates/annual-meeting-agenda/

Tennenbaum, B. November 26, 2016. "How Much Should I Pay the Directors on my Board?" *Forbes*. Forbes.com

Tsao, C.W., M.J. Wang, C.M. Lu, and Y.H. Wang. 2018. "Internationalization Propensity in Family-Controlled Public Firms in Emerging Markets." *Journal of Small Business Strategy*, [S.l.], 28, no. 1, pp. 28–37. http://libjournals.mtsu.edu/index.php/jsbs/article/view/1078

Van Aaken, D., K. Rost, and D. Seidl. 2017. "The Substitution of Governance Mechanisms in the Evolution of Family Firms." *Long Range Planning* 50, pp. 826–39

Waldkirch, M. 2015. "Social Identity Theory and the Family Business." In *Theoretical Perspectives on Family Businesses,* eds. M. Nordqvist, L. Melin, M. Waldkirch, and G. Kumeto. Cheltenham, UK: Edward Elgar Publishing, pp. 137–55. doi:10.4337/9781783479665.00015

Wang, Y. 2010. A report on the IFERA@CHINA 2010 Family Business Forum: Opportunities and challenges of family business. Wolverhampton, UK: Wolverhampton Business School, on behalf of IFERA@CHINA.

Ward, J.L. 1986. *Keeping the Family Business Healthy.* New York, NY: Jossey-Bass.

Ward, J.L. 1987. *Keeping the Family Business Healthy.* New York, NY: Jossey-Bass.

Ward, J.L. 1988. "The Active Board with Outside Directors and the Family Firm." *Family Business Review* 1, pp. 223–229.

Ward, J.L. 2003. "Good Governance is Different for Family Firms." *Families in Business* 2, no. 1, pp. 84–85.

Welsch, J. 1996. *The Best of FBR: A celebration.* Boston, MA: Family Firm Institute, pp. 96–108.

Wilson, N., M. Wright, and L. Scholes. 2017. "Family Business Survival and the Role of Boards." *Entrepreneurship Theory and Practice*37, no. 6, pp. 1369–1389.

Zellweger, T.M., K.A. Eddleston, and F.W. Kellermanns. 2010. "Exploring the Concept of Familiness: Introducing Family Firm Identity." *Journal of Family Business Strategy* 1, no. 1, pp. 54–63.

About the Author

Keanon J. Alderson holds an MBA and a PhD in organization and management. He is a professor of management at California Baptist University in the Robert K. Jabs School of Business where he teaches a family business management course. His research has been published in the *Thunderbird International Business Review*, the *Journal of Family Business Management*, *Family Business Magazine*, and his own book *Understanding the Family Business: Exploring the Differences between Family and Non-family Firms*, by Business Expert Press (2018). He has contributed five chapters to collected volumes. He has presented to numerous audiences and is in demand as a speaker. He consults with family-owned firms on succession, developing an effective board, corporate and family governance, preventing conflict, decision making, and increasing the professionalism and effectiveness of family owned firms.

Index

148   INDEX

OTHER TITLES IN THE ENTREPRENEURSHIP AND SMALL BUSINESS MANAGEMENT COLLECTION

Scott Shane, Case Western University, *Editor*

- *African American Entrepreneurs: Successes and Struggles of Entrepreneurs of Color in America* by Michelle Ingram Spain and J. Mark Munoz
- *How to Get Inside Someone's Mind and Stay There: The Small Business Owner's Guide to Content Marketing and Effective Message Creation* by Jacky Fitt
- *Profit: Plan for It, Get It—The Entrepreneurs Handbook* by H.R. Hutter
- *Navigating Entrepreneurship: 11 Proven Keys to Success* by Larry Jacobson
- *Global Women in the Start-up World: Conversations in Silicon Valley* by Marta Zucker
- *Understanding the Family Business: Exploring the Differences Between Family and Nonfamily Businesses, Second Edition* by Keanon J. Alderson
- *Growth-Oriented Entrepreneurship* by Alan S. Gutterman
- *Founders* by Alan S. Gutterman
- *Entrepreneurship* by Alan S. Gutterman
- *Sustainable Entrepreneurship* by Alan S. Gutterman
- *Startup Strategy Humor: Democratizing Startup Strategy* by Rajesh K. Pillania
- *The Leadership Development Journey: How Entrepreneurs Develop Leadership Through Their Lifetime* by Jen Vuhuong
- *Getting to Market With Your MVP: How to Achieve Small Business and Entrepreneur Success* by J.C. Baker
- *Can You Run Your Business With Blood, Sweat, and Tears? Volume I: Blood* by Stephen Elkins-Jarrett and Nick Skinner
- *Can You Run Your Business With Blood, Sweat, and Tears? Volume II: Sweat* by Stephen Elkins-Jarrett and Nick Skinner
- *Can You Run Your Business With Blood, Sweat, and Tears? Volume III: Tear* by Stephen Elkins-Jarrett and Nick Skinner

Announcing the Business Expert Press Digital Library

Concise e-books business students need for classroom and research

This book can also be purchased in an e-book collection by your library as

- a one-time purchase,
- that is owned forever,
- allows for simultaneous readers,
- has no restrictions on printing, and
- can be downloaded as PDFs from within the library community.

Our digital library collections are a great solution to beat the rising cost of textbooks. E-books can be loaded into their course management systems or onto students' e-book readers.

The **Business Expert Press** digital libraries are very affordable, with no obligation to buy in future years. For more information, please visit **www.businessexpertpress.com/librarians**. To set up a trial in the United States, please email **sales@businessexpertpress.com**.

www.ingramcontent.com/pod-product-compliance
Lightning Source LLC
Chambersburg PA
CBHW061317220326
41599CB00026B/4928